Crowd Control

Crowd Management and Effective Teaching for Chorus, Band, and Orchestra

Second Edition

Susan L. Haugland

Published in partnership with
National Association for Music Education

ROWMAN & LITTLEFIELD EDUCATION
A division of
ROWMAN & LITTLEFIELD PUBLISHERS, INC.
Lanham • New York • Toronto • Plymouth, UK

Published in partnership with National Association for Music Education

Published by Rowman & Littlefield Education
A division of Rowman & Littlefield Publishers, Inc.
A wholly owned subsidiary of The Rowman & Littlefield Publishing Group, Inc.
4501 Forbes Boulevard, Suite 200, Lanham, Maryland 20706
www.rowman.com

10 Thornbury Road, Plymouth PL6 7PP, United Kingdom

British Library Cataloguing in Publication Information Available

Library of Congress Cataloging-in-Publication Data

Haugland, Susan L.
Crowd control : crowd management and effective teaching for chorus, band, and orchestra / Susan L. Haugland. — Second edition.
pages cm
"Published in partnership with National Association for Music Education."
ISBN 978-1-4758-0362-4 (cloth : alk. paper) — ISBN 978-1-4758-0363-1 (pbk. : alk. paper) — ISBN 978-1-4758-0364-8 (electronic)
1. School music—Instruction and study. 2. Classroom management. I. National Association for Music Education. II. Title.
MT1.H38 2013
781.44071'2—dc23
2012046634

The paper used in this publication meets the minimum requirements of American National Standard for Information Sciences Permanence of Paper for Printed Library Materials, ANSI/NISO Z39.48-1992.

Printed in the United States of America

Contents

Foreword v
Acknowledgments vii
Introduction ix

1 Setting Up Your Plan 1
2 Setting the Plan in Motion 17
3 Following Your Plan 25
4 Creating a Team 33
5 Projects, Process, and Purpose 43
6 Advocacy 53
7 Assessment 59

Appendix A: Sample Choral Handbook 69
Appendix B: Sample Blank Checkbook Page 73
Appendix C: Ideas for Student Projects 75
Appendix D: Sample Rubrics 77
Appendix E: Resources 81
About the Author 83

Foreword

Yes, there are other resources—books, articles, and online resources—that address classroom management. But what Susan Haugland brings to us is a unique blend of her personal experience and down-to-earth attitude.

As a music teacher, you know that rehearsal time is a precious commodity, and making the most of it by running an efficient classroom that maximizes learning and minimizes interruptions is a vital part of providing your pupils with high-quality music instruction.

The reader will quickly realize that her casual, witty style contains a great deal of valuable information based on solid success within a variety of media, age groups, and environments. Just her advice on how to get ready for the first day is worth the cost of this book.

Written as though you were chatting with her in a local coffee shop or teachers' lounge, Susan has a knack for knowing what makes students—especially middle school students—tick. She presents tons of good information within a practical framework that accurately reflects what real music classrooms and, more importantly, what real students are actually like.

I am confident that *Crowd Control* will engender can-do confidence in preservice and first-year teachers, as well as assuage some of those first-day through first-year jitters. Experienced teachers will likewise gain a new perspective on familiar, ongoing challenges, such as fundraising while also building ensemble unity, assessing student achievement aligned with the National Standards for Music Education, motivating students, infusing fresh air into an established program, and staving off burnout and stagnation.

As I read this book, I often found myself smiling. Susan's keen observations about working with kids, parents, administrators, and school staff will certainly resonate with seasoned teachers. And to save young teachers particular miseries, Susan candidly shares her own mistakes—and explains exactly what to do differently.

I also read *Crowd Control* with a certain amount of regret. Had I read this book years ago, I would have saved all the money that I spent on antacids during my first year of teaching!

I look forward to adopting *Crowd Control* for my instrumental methods classes at Northwestern and will confidently recommend it to my colleagues as well. Now, if you will excuse me, I have to prepare for my next class. . . .

Dr. James Kjelland
Associate Professor of Music Education
Northwestern University

Acknowledgments

I am indebted to numerous teachers from whom I have learned pedagogy; colleagues from whom I have stolen teaching ideas; and students who have endured my many mistakes along the way. I would also like to thank my friends, Mary Shanley and Beth Terrell, and my mother, Linda Lott, for helping me fine-tune my ideas, as well as my editor, Ashley Opp, for putting such elegant finishing touches on this book.

Introduction

I'm writing this book because it occurred to me that, after twenty-three years of teaching, my college education prepared me with almost everything I needed to know about what to teach my students but nothing practical about how to manage my class so that all of those important activities could happen in a productive manner. I did learn important skills such as conducting an orchestra and scheduling lessons, but the "how-to" of managing performance-based classes was woefully missing from my college curriculum.

Many books are available on classroom management for general education teachers, but performance-based classes are unique in several ways. First of all, classes such as band, chorus, and orchestra typically have a higher student-to-teacher ratio than average classes. The sixth-grade band at my school now has ninety-six members. That's a 96:1 student-to-teacher ratio! You'd better have a really good management system in place in order to make a class like that work. If you don't, you'll spend very little of your class time on actual instruction.

While English, math, and science are required classes, band, chorus, and orchestra are probably not. Students are not placed in your class—they join your organization. Unlike regular education teachers, recruiting students is a part of your job. You're not only a teacher; you're also a salesperson. You have to sell your program to students and parents, and, more importantly, you have to sell yourself as a teacher. If your class is run poorly, word will get out. You won't be able to recruit as many students, and your class sizes will decrease. This puts your program in jeopardy of getting cut back or eliminated altogether.

Typically, a core-curriculum teacher has a one-year relationship with his or her students. Band, chorus, and orchestra teachers, however, may see their students over a period of many years. Most of us teach several grade levels. Once you establish a behavior plan in your class, students will know what to expect from year to year. You'll spend less time enforcing the plan after the first year, allowing for higher-quality instructional time. After years of trial and error, I settled on a system that makes my classes run smoothly and allows me to focus more on teaching and less on discipline.

During our years in college, we learned a variety of theoretical approaches to teaching music, formed lofty idealistic goals for our careers, and even practiced teaching—with other college students as our class.

Now that's a realistic experience, isn't it? When we did venture out to schools, we had a seasoned teacher right behind us. When my first real teaching job landed me in front of a 140-member choir in a school largely populated by the nearby housing projects in Peoria, Illinois, I quickly realized that I was not very well prepared for the task before me.

Not only was I not teaching orchestra, my area of concentration in school, but I was also teaching in a gymnasium with my 140 students sitting on bleachers. I was hired three days before school started, and I didn't even have a class list. I had no desk, no music, no accompanist, and no idea what to do. Nothing I had learned in college could be applied to this group of children. Not knowing what else to do, I taught them "The Lion Sleeps Tonight." They loved it, and it got me through that first day, after which I went home and lost a lot of sleep trying to figure out what I should do the next day.

Fast-forward twenty-one years: I'm teaching chorus once again in a small but growing town in northern Illinois. I replaced a teacher whose reputation for having a very relaxed method of teaching attracted a large number of students who were more interested in relaxing than singing. Needless to say, the seventh and eighth graders who encountered my expectations on the first day of school were not very happy. They did everything they could to make my life miserable that first year. Out of that misery came the ideas and plans that I'm going to share with you.

Please don't use these plans exactly as written. Every school, every classroom, every group of students is different, and you'll have to adapt the ideas in this book to fit your style and surroundings. Some of the thoughts in the following chapters will work for you just as they are, some will need some adaptation, and some won't work at all. You might think that something will work but, after trying it, realize it's not right for your classroom—or you will find the opposite to be true. Keep what works and throw out what doesn't.

I would love to hear what works for you, what doesn't, and any new ideas you have. After all, I've stolen ideas from every good teacher I've ever observed, and you should do the same.

ONE

Setting Up Your Plan

Setting up your plan includes the routines, procedures, and everything else you have to figure out before you can actually teach.

BEFORE THE FIRST DAY OF SCHOOL—GRADE BOOKS AND SEATING CHARTS

If you're lucky, you'll be hired more than three days before the start of school, but even if that's all the time you have, you still have time to be successful.

First, your school should provide you with a grade book and a class list; if they don't, ask. Fill out the grade book with the students' names down the left side and the dates across the top. That's the obvious thing to do, I guess, but I didn't know that when I got my first job.

Next, you need to take a really good look at your classroom. Do you actually have a classroom, or do you teach in the gym or cafeteria? Where will the students sit or stand—on chairs, risers . . . bleachers? Where will you stand? If you teach chorus, do you have an accompanist? Or do you stand behind the piano like I do?

The layout of your classroom is crucial to your success. You need to be able to see each and every student in your class. Before the students arrive on the first day, decide where each and every student will sit or stand.

After you fill out your grade book and look at your classroom, create a blank seating chart for your classroom. Make copies of it, because you'll be changing it from time to time. Since, generally speaking, bands, orchestras, and choirs don't have desks in rows, just draw squares in the arrangement that you intend to have students sit or stand.

My seating chart is simply three horizontal rows of squares on a piece of paper. I have fifty-five students in my largest class, so I drew sixty squares. I use the same chart for all of my classes; I just have more empty squares for the smaller groups.

You might think that sixty squares would most easily be arranged as twenty squares in each of three rows. When the rows are curved, though, fewer chairs fit on the bottom row than on the top row. That's why I put fifteen on the bottom row, twenty on the middle row, and twenty-five on the top row. You may need more rows than I do, but I'd rather have my students spread from side to side than front to back. My classroom is designed so that if I put students on the top level of the built-in risers, they're very far away from me. It's just one more logistic to consider when you're surveying your kingdom.

When students come in the room for the very first time, one of the first things they want to know is where they belong. You'd better be prepared with a seating chart before they arrive—even if you have to change it immediately because the boy you put in the middle of the bottom row is six foot two and the girl in the top row is four foot one.

If you teach band or orchestra, you have the advantage of knowing what instruments students play most of the time, which takes a lot of the guesswork out of the seating chart. Whether or not to test for chairs is an entirely different issue (though related to seating), and I'll bet they taught you in college about the different theories regarding that subject, so I'll leave that one up to you. In the beginning, though, you put the names on the chart and tell them to sit there.

If you had these students the previous year, you should know who can sit next to whom and not cause problems. If not, it doesn't hurt to ask their former classroom teachers for advice. Students invariably insist that they can sit next to their best friend and still pay adequate attention to the instruction taking place in class. They're wrong. You're the teacher—you decide where they sit.

You should consider a few other items before the first day of class, such as where your students should put their things when they are in your room. It may not seem important now, but if you have ninety-six students coming in your room, space is probably tight already. Those kids likely have notebooks, textbooks, purses, and who knows what else. Where would you like to store these things during class so no one trips over all that stuff? I have my students put everything under their chairs, but there might be a better solution for your classroom. This is something you want to let your students know on the first day of class; otherwise, bad habits will start immediately. Middle schoolers in particular are notorious for dropping things right inside the doorway or other inconvenient locations. Encourage good habits right from the beginning.

Are safety plans posted clearly in your classroom? If not, you need to check with the office and get a map of exit plans for your room with instructions about what to do in case of fire or tornado (or hurricane, earthquake, nuclear disaster, or whatever potential disaster might happen in your location). Since the Columbine shootings, many schools also have created plans for this type of emergency, known only to the faculty. If you do not receive this information, make sure to ask. Often a teacher thinks about safety plans for the first time only when the school has a drill. Make sure your room has exit plans posted and know what they are. Make absolutely that sure your students know what to do before an actual emergency happens.

Before school starts, you should think about what supplies your students need for class. Obviously, if you're an instrumental teacher, they need an instrument, but they might need other supplies as well. Do they need a folder, or do you have a music store that supplies those for band and orchestra students? I require my chorus students to bring a vinyl folder and a box of tissues (the school does not provide these) to class the first day.

Does your school have choir folders for music? I require my kids to have a pencil in their folder at all times. Would you like them to keep an assignment or other notebook? Make a list of the supplies your students should have and give the office a copy so they can add it to the supply lists that they give out at registration. If your school has supply lists on a website, make sure that the technology department has your list.

Band and orchestra teachers have supplies necessary for all students as well as those that are specific to different instruments. Some directors charge a flat fee for supplies such as folders, method books, lyres, and so on. If you intend to have incidental supplies available for purchase at school (such as reeds, valve oil, strings, rosin), then you should check and see if an instrumental music sales or service person can regularly visit your school and figure out how to set that up. You may need to do purchase orders for those supplies and have students reimburse the school for the cost. If you have a predecessor or if your district has other directors, find out how they handle supplies for band and orchestra so that you don't have to reinvent the wheel.

All of these things need to be thought about, and then you can plan what you're going to teach.

ROOM ORGANIZATION AND DÉCOR

Here are a few thoughts on classroom aesthetics: If your classroom looks disorganized, students assume that you are disorganized, and they will try their best to take advantage of your disorganization. Middle school and high school students will do anything they can to throw you off track and avoid doing actual work. If your classroom has no visible organization, your students will suspect there's no organization in your lesson plans either. Could they be right?

First, you need to plan for instrument and music storage and make labels to show clearly where everything belongs. Unless you're in a brand-new building, it probably has some accommodations for storing instruments, but you need to decide how best to use that storage. Do you want the instruments placed on shelves according to grade level or class as well as by instrument? How will the flow of students in and out of the storage area work? If you're lucky enough to have an instrument storage room with a door at either end, designate one door as the "in" door and the other as the "out" door and enforce it. Students get to their seats faster if they're not bumping into each other—and you have more instructional time. If your storage units are right in the classroom, great, but you still need to label the shelves or lockers according to what they should hold.

Music storage is another big issue. Music is too expensive to risk losing because of disorganization. Always file loose music immediately. Students can help with this. I've found that kids love to have jobs in my classroom. You can designate a couple of librarians for each class. Have them come in one day before or after school, or to eat lunch in your room, and teach them how to file music in score order. Recognize them both in your concert programs and with an award at the end of the year for helping you. Whatever you do, though, don't let music get scattered around your classroom. If someone in your class accidentally leaves a sheet of music on the floor, pick it up and file it right away. When they look for it the next time they play, you'll know where to find it.

With music, I number each part and record the number next to the receiving student's name in my grade book. If they do not return their copy of the music when a concert is finished, or if it is lost or "stolen" during the course of the year, I charge them for the piece of music they lost. All students must have the required pieces of music in their folder at every rehearsal. Some of them try to pretend that they're looking at music when it's not really there, but it's pretty easy to catch them. If the music isn't back in their folder by the next rehearsal, they are charged for it. I communicate all of this to parents in the handbook, at parent meetings, on curriculum nights, and on my website.

I order roughly ten more copies of the music than the estimated number of students in my class so that no student has to go too long without the required piece in his or her folder. If the kid who loses the music has to cough up the money for a new copy, that student learns pretty quickly to take care of his or her music.

Keep your scores in order and in the same place all the time. You want to teach your kids to keep track of their music, right? Set a good example by doing that yourself. If you can't find your music, you waste instructional time looking for it and you chip away at the respect your students have for you because you appear disorganized.

If the furnishings in your room are not sufficient to store everything you need efficiently, use some of your budget to purchase storage containers, paper trays, baskets, and so on. If everything has a designated place, less is lost and you save money in the long run. Visit other teachers who teach what you teach and see how they store their stuff.

The courses you teach dictate the furniture you need in your room, but almost all instrumental or choral teachers need a desk, several file cabinets, bookshelves, music folder storage for students, a podium, a piano, chairs, and music stands. Instrumental teachers need well-organized instrument storage. If you're lucky enough to design a room from scratch, seek the assistance of a company that manufactures equipment for instrumental music. They will design plans for you free of charge in the hope that you will purchase the furnishings from them.

In, on, and around my desk, I keep my computer, phone, office supplies, grade book, lesson plans, seating chart, and calendar. On top of my desk I have a standing file holding instructions for a substitute teacher. The office area of my classroom has shelves and drawers for band instrument supplies that are for sale, and also for those items necessary to maintain and repair instruments. Make sure those supplies can be locked up, or they will disappear.

In the filing cabinets not easily accessible by students, I file music alphabetically by title and according to grade level or voicing (SA, SSA, SATB, three-part mixed). I also keep a file with folders containing all the past programs (so we don't repeat music too often), notes that I sent home regarding contests and performances, information on district festivals, assessment rubrics, project ideas, and worksheets. It's much easier to copy or rework existing documents than to create new ones, and sometimes it's difficult from year to year to remember what you did for different events. Lots of these documents are probably stored on your computer as well, but you never know what the tech department is going to do with your computer over the summer, so it's a good idea to keep hard copies too.

I spent three years trying to figure out the best way to store the music we were actively singing. First, I had students keep their music in folders in the classroom in folder slots assigned to them. Almost every day someone would tell me that someone else "stole" his or her music. The next year, I moved the folder slots to a spot right next to my office, thinking it would be less likely to disappear, but disappear it did. Finally, I asked another chorus teacher friend of mine what he did, and he had been through exactly the same trial-and-error process that I had. He told me that he just gave the students the music to keep until after the concerts and made it their responsibility not to lose it. They actually took the music home and practiced it! What a concept! I tried that the next year, and it worked for me too. It's amazing what you learn if you just ask.

If you recruited students in the spring of the previous year or over the summer, you probably have a pretty good idea of how many students you can expect in each class in the fall. If not, you have to wait until class lists are ready. Either way, you need to start to plan the layout of your room as soon as you know who will be in your class. Several different ensembles will probably use your room throughout the day. If your school is like mine, you're not the only teacher using the room. Work together with your colleagues to decide where to place furniture such as chairs, stands, tables, and storage units. Decide who will move chairs and stands to accommodate the different groups that will be using the room. You will probably have to make adjustments to this plan after the first week, but it's much easier to adjust an existing plan than to start from scratch later.

A side note here: I suggest you not allow students to move furniture unless you have asked them to. I've had students decide they like this or that chair better because it has a little gray mark on the corner. They want to come in, inspect every chair in the room until they find that chair with the little gray mark, and then move it to their assigned spot. Nope. Not in my classroom they don't. They're wasting valuable instructional time. Students may not move furniture unless I ask them to move furniture.

Now that you have your room organized and ready to go, you can put some thought into the décor. I'm not talking *Better Homes and Gardens* here; I'm talking about creating a room that's an attractive, interesting place to learn. Remember, a few decorations make the room cheerful; too many make it distracting. Put lesson schedules, concert dates, and so on in a central location and add a border around it to draw attention to the importance of these items. Posters, motivational or decorative, should be hung high on the walls so they are visible but not a point of focus. You should be the point of focus. If the posters are in the same line of vision as you are, they will distract your students.

Bulletin boards are a great place to teach students more about the concepts they're studying. If you're a bulletin board kind of person, you can enrich your curriculum by creating a center where students can find additional information about the music they're playing or singing. Change them often so they remain interesting, and students will look forward to seeing new displays. If you're not a bulletin board kind of person, you might fill your bulletin board once a year with visuals of fundamentals so students know where they can look for basic information. For example, a chart could explain commonly used music terms or key signatures or rhythms.

When decorating your room, remember that students respect their surroundings more if they feel they, themselves, are respected. This means preparing an inviting place for them to learn. Overall, the room layout should communicate to students the purpose of the class. Put up decorations specific to what you teach. If you crowd your walls with posters of kittens and puppies, it detracts from your lessons.

My current classroom had not been repainted since the school was built over fifty years ago—a nauseating shade of very ripe banana. The room had "acoustic" tiles (they were really drop-ceiling tiles) nailed around the perimeter of the room just below the ceiling, but they had suffered many years of pencil tossing and were very sad-looking. The room had eighty chairs (I share the room with the band director), and no more than five were the same color or type. If the room contained a music stand that stood perpendicular to the floor, I couldn't find it. The room, located over the boiler room, has only one very small window for ventilation and no air conditioning. The piano, which was probably once a beautiful instrument, was miraculously still standing upright after years of abuse and poor climate, though it didn't hold a tune.

I couldn't do much before the first day that first year besides putting up some posters and cleaning up the neglected mess. However, the second year, we organized a Music Room Makeover Day. Parents came in with 30 gallons of paint and 210 yards of burlap. The school district agreed to pay for the paint and fabric if we could find willing laborers. We painted the room in fresh, clean, white paint and covered the ceiling tiles—excuse me, acoustic tiles—with burlap fabric. We held a fundraiser so we could purchase some Wenger chairs. It wasn't much, but it made a huge difference in how the students felt when they came into the room the following Monday. We bought new stands and a few more chairs the next year, and the Music Boosters helped us purchase a new Clavinova, which could withstand the climate of the room better than an acoustic piano could.

If you have a Music Boosters organization already in place in your school, get to know them. If not, organize a group. The National Association for Music Education (NAfME) has excellent resources available to help you organize a boosters group. Music Boosters can raise funds for expenditures beyond the scope of your school budget, such as special trips, awards, or equipment. The group can also help to publicize the benefits of your program. Advocacy is vital to the future of our field, and Music Boosters can be your biggest supporters. The Music Boosters at my school help purchase badly needed new equipment, but members also set up for concerts, chaperone trips, and work tirelessly on the high school musical.

The chosen décor for the fresh new space included a few motivational posters, lesson schedules, and some personal pictures of the teachers on the bulletin board (so the kids don't think we live at school). We have also put up a T-shirt from each of the Broadway musicals we've attended (I'll tell you more about that later).

You may not think you have the resources to change your classroom if it needs help. If you change how you're thinking, though, you might find a way. I never worked in a school district with so little money available, but we found ways to make our space a better place for learning. As a result, the students respect us more because they know that we care enough about them to provide the best possible environment.

THE BATHROOM AND THE DRINKING FOUNTAIN

Before school starts, check with the rest of the faculty and administration to see what kind of policy, if any, is in place for granting bathroom and drink privileges. If there's a school-wide policy, stick to it unless an obvious emergency occurs. If a school-wide policy is not in place, then you're on your own. You better have a plan before your first class, or you'll do nothing but hand out hall passes.

In my building, students have three minutes' passing time between classes. I was curious, so I actually timed myself going from one class to a locker, and then to another classroom on another side of the building. It took me four minutes, and I didn't stop at the drinking fountain or the bathroom. Granted, I'm a few years older than my students, and I wear dress shoes, not running shoes, but there's no way, in my opinion, that they have enough time to empty their bladder except at lunchtime. No eighth-grade teacher allows students to use the restroom during class, and my class is their last one before lunch. When my eighth-grade students arrive in my classroom at 10:20, most of them have not used the restroom since they left home—and some of them leave home at 6:30 a.m. I believe them, for the most part, when they say they need to use the bathroom.

In order to keep learning time as interruption-free as possible, I instituted my own policy. I write bathroom passes during the first five minutes of class when I'm taking attendance and making announcements. After that, they need to wait until lunchtime. I don't allow anyone to go to the drinking fountain, though, unless they have a serious case of the hiccups or they're coughing up a lung. I do, however, allow them to bring bottles of water into my classroom.

I only let students out of the room one at a time. This prevents potty parties in the restroom and ensures a speedy return to the classroom. To this end, I have a bathroom pass that the students must physically carry to the bathroom. My pass is a large plastic case that held a set of LPs in its former life, and it's marked in large, bold letters: "Mrs. Haugland's Bathroom Pass." It's hard to lose and easily visible to other staff members in case the student who should be in the bathroom loses his or her way and finds him- or herself in another part of the building. If that should happen, any staff member who sees the pass in the student's hand may assume that the student is lost and needs directions back to my classroom, possibly with a detention slip.

Decide on your own policy before the first day of school and stick to it (unless it's completely unreasonable and needs to be changed). If you change your policy for one student, you have to change it for all of them—and you'll end up with no policy at all.

THE BEHAVIOR PLAN

Now, on to the really important point of this book: the behavior plan. Some schools have a consistent discipline plan across different grade levels. Ours does not. Frankly, it doesn't matter what plan the school has; this plan works alongside whatever the school has in place, whether it's good, bad, or nonexistent. As you may have realized, your class is different from almost every other class in the building, and it helps to have a behavior plan designed specifically to work for you.

One of the unique things about teaching a performance-based class is that you will likely have the students for their entire stay at your school, whether it's elementary, middle, or high school, or perhaps even a combination of two or more of those schools. Most classroom teachers only see students for one year; you may have them in class for several years. If your behavior plan stays the same for every grade level you teach, the students will be comfortable with it. Even if the discipline plan outside your class changes from year to year, your students know what you expect from them and what they can expect from you.

This plan evolved out of a merit and demerit system, but it is easier to manage since it doesn't require printing of merits or demerits. I also tie it into my grading system. It's simple, easy to use, and works for every grade I've ever taught—even high school.

In appendix B, you will find a sample of the chart I use for my behavior plan. I fill in the names of the students in the class down the left side, and I fill in the titles of the columns with behaviors I want to see from each student (some classes take up two or more pages).

I include the following behaviors on my chart:

1. In seat when the bell rings
2. Is prepared for class with all materials necessary
3. Demonstrates proper posture when playing or singing
4. Is quiet during rehearsal when not playing or singing
5. Shows respect for self and others
6. Participates appropriately during rehearsal
7. Goes above and beyond

My personal opinion is that when these behaviors are stated in a positive manner, rather than in a negative way, students know what is expected of them on a daily basis. Not only are these behaviors in my "checkbook," but they are also posted on the wall in my classroom.

After the blank forms have been filled out with students' names and behaviors, make enough copies so that you have one copy for each class for each week of the year, quarter, or semester. Three-hole punch the pages and put them in a binder. This is your "checkbook." I also use colored dividers between each class so I can easily flip from one class to the next when students arrive in my room.

On the first day of class, fill in "week of August 20" (or whatever week it is) at the top of the first form for each class. When students do not demonstrate one of these behaviors, I simply point at them, then they walk quietly over and put their initials in the box that applies to the rule they have violated. Sometimes they ask which behavior it was, but they usually know. They have to write small in case they have another problem with that same behavior in the same week.

Don't put the checkbook on the opposite side of the room from where you stand. Believe it or not, students sometimes only pretend to write their initials in the box. You can't believe it, can you? Well, it's true. You need to be able to see them write their initials, and you need to have a pen attached to the checkbook for them to use because pencil gets erased and, if you don't attach the pen, it will disappear. Again, hard to believe, isn't it? (I have the book right under my nose so I can watch them write their initials in the correct box.)

The last column on the right is the "above and beyond" category. This column is where I ask them to write their initials if they did something that was extra wonderful. I give out above and beyond rewards for moving more stands than I asked them to, picking up someone else's garbage, singing or playing with particular passion, showing extra care or politeness to someone in the room, helping set up for a concert, and so on.

Now, what do you do with all those initials in the boxes at the end of the week? I'll tell you what I do, and you can adapt it to fit your situation. For one check—that's one set of initials in a box for an entire week—I subtract five points from their quarterly grade. For two checks, I subtract ten points from their quarterly grade, and they become ineligible for our weekly Monday morning drawing, which I will explain in a moment. For three checks, I subtract twenty-five points from the student's quarterly grade, and the student receives an after-school detention. If a student receives more than three checks in a single week, I have a parent-student-teacher conference.

Students who receive checks in the "above and beyond" category can erase a check from another category, or, if they have received no check marks in other categories, they get to enter the Monday morning prize drawing twice.

Every Monday morning, every student with zero or one check writes their name on a little piece of scrap paper, and I draw two names from each class. These students get to pick a prize out of a big jar. I have items in the prize jar like gel pens, candy bars, highlighters, sticky pads, or anything else I can find cheap at dollar stores. I teach three classes, so I give away six items a week. So far I've paid for these items myself because I don't have a budget for it, but you could ask parents to send things in for the prize jar. I figure it costs me about $2 a week. Not a high price to pay for good behavior, in my experience.

At the end of the week, I record all the grade points lost and all of the detentions I need to write up. I then clip the page to the rest of the pages that have already been used, open to a fresh form, and write the date for the next week at the top.

It's essential that you have this plan developed before the first day of school so you can explain it fully to the students on the first day and give it to them in written form in the handbook you give them to survive in your class.

THE HANDBOOK

My handbook contains all the vital information that students and parents need to know in order to be successful in my class. This includes the following:

1. Dates for all the required concerts for the year and an outline of optional activities
2. The behavior plan and consequences for violations
3. Grading procedures
4. Concert dress
5. Importance of music in education
6. Importance of participation in all concerts
7. For band or orchestra, possibly accessory price lists and scheduling information
8. A form for parents and students to sign and return, stating that they have read and understood all of the information in the handbook

Concert dates are the first item that the parents see when they open the handbook. It clearly states the importance of attending and participating in each and every concert and reminds parents to put the concert dates on their home calendars immediately so that families can schedule appointments and other things around them. Vacations, doctor appointments, and guests visiting from out of town do not constitute excused absences. If the student was sick on the day of the concert, he or she is excused but must do a makeup assignment.

I outline the behavior plan and the consequences and follow it immediately with my grading plan. More details on rubrics, assessments, and grading can be found in a later chapter, but for now, I'll tell you that I give each student five hundred points each quarter.

Students receive five points for each rehearsal. I don't refer to our daily meeting as "class." I call it a rehearsal, just as the professionals do. I let my students know that they are musicians on day one, and musicians rehearse. This communicates my expectation of professional behavior in the room. With approximately forty class periods in each quarter, the rehearsal points total two hundred each grading period. If a student receives a check on any given day, he or she loses all five grade points for that day.

Each required concert is worth two hundred points, and we have one concert each quarter. If students do not show up in concert dress, they lose fifty points. If they are absent with an invalid excuse, they lose all two hundred points. If the student was absent from school on the day of the performance due to illness, or if his or her parents call me the day after the performance to let me know that their child was sick, that's an excused absence. I don't accept notes for this; I must have a phone call from a parent.

Missing a performance to attend any event that could have been scheduled on a nonattendance day is unexcused. I've had parents send in all of the following excuses that were unexcused according to my policy: vacations, eye doctor and dentist appointments, babysitting for younger siblings, and even trips to the mall. Your students need to understand your policy, but, more importantly, their parents need to understand it as well. If your attendance policy is clearly defined in the handbook (which parents must sign), then you have the upper hand when a parent approaches you to argue about his or her child's grade and how it was affected by a missed performance.

Unprofessional behavior at a performance can also cost students points. Knowing how to behave in a performance is an important fundamental we learn in class. The actual performance is the means of evaluating this learning objective. Talking during a performance, eyes wandering from the director, poor posture, eye-rolling, or refusal to play or sing all exemplify unprofessional performance behavior. Rubrics help evaluate performance behavior (examples can be found in appendix D).

In addition to daily rehearsal points and performance points, I designate one hundred points each quarter for a quiz, written assignment, or play test. I do sight-singing quizzes and some cross-curricular assignments during the year. Four to five hundred points is an A, 300–399 points is a B, and so on.

This is a very concrete way of grading in a very nonconcrete type of class. It's clear and easy to understand and provides a measure of success for students who are doing their best. It's the grading system I use, and it works for me.

CONCERT DRESS

We tried a few different approaches to concert dress and finally came up with what I like the best. We don't have a budget for uniforms or robes. At one time we had the kids "dress up." That didn't work—there are way too many definitions of "dressing up." Next, we tried white shirts and black bottoms. That didn't work either. There is bright white, winter white, eggshell white, ecru . . . long sleeves, short sleeves, no sleeves, long skirts, and extremely short skirts that caused me to send girls home to change.

Now our concert dress is simple, and I leave no room for discussion. We have a white T-shirt with a left chest logo designed for our music department so the students who take both band and chorus can use the same shirt. They can also use the same shirt all three years they're at our school, provided they buy a big enough shirt in the first place. Our local sporting goods store screen prints the T-shirts for $6 each, and they save the screen so we can order more whenever we need them. The students must wear that shirt tucked into (and they whine about that) black pants—long pants, not capri pants. They must have black shoes and black socks. Goodwill has a huge selection of black shoes and pants, and I send kids there regularly to get what they need for concerts.

Everyone looks uniform, neat, and tidy; we feel like a team, and no one had to shell out a ton of money.

CONCERT DATES

I schedule one required performance for each grading quarter during the school year. If you're new to the district, your concert dates may already be scheduled before you even arrive. If not, you probably should check and see how many and when the concerts were scheduled the previous year and keep the same basic schedule your first year. You can make adjustments after you see how prepared or unprepared you were for those performances with the number of rehearsals you have during the week.

In addition to concerts, we have an organizational contest, a solo and ensemble contest, and a district festival. You need to decide if those events will be required or not, based on the amount of time you have to spend with students. Our organizational contest is required, but solo and ensemble events and district festival auditions are optional for students.

I post the concert dates in the handbook, on our school website, and in our classroom. It's also a good idea to send press releases to the local newspapers a few weeks in advance. The more you keep your organization in the public eye, the more support you will have for your program.

THE PURPOSE OF THE ENSEMBLE

The NAfME National Standards 1 and 2 state that students need to be "singing, alone and with others, a varied repertoire of music [and] performing on instruments, alone and with others, a varied repertoire of music." A performance-based class naturally meets this standard for teaching music. Beyond that, the benefits are many.

When students rehearse together and perform together as a team, they develop their interpersonal intelligence. According to educational psychologist Howard Gardner, people with developed interpersonal intelligence have the ability to work together in groups toward common goals and establish positive relationships with others. They also have skills in conflict resolution and recognize strengths of other team members. Music performance teaches students to think creatively and solve problems. These skills will benefit students, no matter what they choose to do with the rest of their lives.

Through the discipline of music, students improve cognitive, communication, and study skills, all of which transfer to other areas of the curriculum. New research comes out all the time suggesting a relationship between the study of music and higher test scores in other academic areas. The high school in our district compared the average ACT scores of last year's music students with students not taking music classes and found that, on average, the music students scored higher than students not in music. This is powerful information to bring to the attention of parents and the school board when the need to justify your program arises.

Music performance teaches students to overcome anxiety and to take risks. They learn poise, composure, and the value of continued effort to achieve excellence. Above all, music performance students know the satisfaction of the successful result of hard work, and this carries over into every other aspect of their lives.

Communicate these and other benefits, such as lower incidences of drug and alcohol use and higher levels of self-esteem, to parents, administrators, and community members on a regular basis in order to encourage support for the important work you do. NAfME has fantastic resources detailing research concerning the importance of music education (see appendix E).

Explain exactly why your class is important to the students' overall development and why participation in every performance is critical to the success of the entire ensemble. Put it in writing in the handbook and make sure your administrators have a copy.

In the handbook that I send home with my students, I state these reasons for required participation in performances:

- Ensemble performance is a group effort. Every missing member weakens the performance. We rehearse together and we perform together.
- Performing for an audience is the primary focus of our class. Concerts provide an experience that cannot be reproduced in the classroom.
- Performances are the means by which the skills learned in class are assessed by the teacher and comprise the largest percentage of the student's quarterly grade.

OPTIONAL ACTIVITIES

In addition to the four required performances that my ensembles have every year, I give them additional performance opportunities that not only are fun but also help bring more attention to our programs.

While students can enroll in both band and chorus, most do not choose to join both because they lose a study hall. Because of this scheduling problem, I had significantly fewer students in chorus than in band during my first year of teaching in this district. Instruments, of course, are something new for our sixth-grade students, and the lure of the shiny saxophones and flutes is irresistible. They have, after all, been singing since kindergarten, making chorus seem far less intriguing by comparison. In order to add some marketable selling points, I felt the vocal music program needed to get involved in some activities in which the chorus students could participate and band students could not.

One of the easiest and least expensive trips we took was to the mall to sing. The shopping mall in the city closest to our town has a program in which local groups are brought in throughout the holiday season to entertain shoppers. We wear concert dress, but I allow the kids to wear Santa hats and reindeer antlers while performing. I was amazed at how much the students loved this event. Whether or not we would repeat our mall performance was the question at the top of their list when they returned to school the following year.

We also go to a festival competition at Six Flags. This is a more costly trip but well worth the effort it takes to get there. This trip brings us together as a team like nothing else. The added benefit of a day at the theme park is something that has been a great recruiting tool and greatly increased the enrollment in my classes.

I outline these extra activities in the handbook even though I don't always have the exact dates confirmed. This way, parents keep an eye out for information on extra performances.

Extra activities help to create bonding within your ensembles. Children who feel they're part of a team feel that they belong, and that's a really great thing for you and your students.

SIGN IT AND SEND IT BACK

In the center of my handbook there is a page that looks like this:

> ***Important!***
>
> Read and discuss this entire handbook with your child before signing and returning this form.
>
> Please return this signed page to Mrs. Haugland before Friday, August 31. Make sure to keep the concert schedule and mark the dates on your calendar now. If any changes occur, you will be notified as soon as possible.
>
> I have read the choral handbook, and I understand the expectations. If I have any questions or concerns, I will contact Mrs. Haugland.
>
> Student Signature ______________________________
> Parent/Guardian Signature ______________________________

When questions about the grading system, behavior plan, or concert dates come up throughout the year, I can remind parents that they had this information the first week of school and that they signed a paper saying they read and understood the handbook. This doesn't occur very often, but the signature makes it very difficult for a parent or student to dispute any aspects of the program.

The handbook is an essential part of my classroom management system because it involves not only each student but his or her family as well. My principal also has a copy and has approved it, so I know he'll be able to support me if issues arise. I must say, however, that I have had far fewer conflicts since its inception. I have included a complete copy of the handbook in appendix A. Feel free to borrow from it or even copy it verbatim and change the names and dates.

When you have developed your behavior plan, created your seating chart, filled out your grade book, organized your classroom, printed your handbook, and written your lesson plans, you can breathe a sigh of relief because you know that you are ready for the first day of school.

TWO

Setting the Plan in Motion

The teaching success that you have at the end of the year is determined, to a great extent, by what you do in the first few minutes at the beginning of the year. You must implement your plan the very second you first come into contact with your students. I learned this the hard way. Let me save you a year or two of misery.

The last position I held before I started teaching middle school chorus was teaching K–5 general music for eight years. Elementary kids love teachers and have a great desire to please adults. Let me just say that most middle school kids do not have that same desire. I also had been teaching a private youth orchestra of middle school students for several years, so I thought I had it down. Wrong. Different setting, different kids.

I was used to kids who liked me and who did what I asked them to do because they wanted to. When I stepped in front of my class of eighty-six seventh and eighth graders, I was shocked to learn that most of them took the class because they expected to have the previous teacher, who required very little of them. They didn't expect me, and they weren't happy. They were also not shy about expressing their displeasure. The rebellious behavior took different forms. A few really bold kids shouted some nasty things at me. Many of them sat stone-faced and quiet in their chairs, arms folded in front of them, refusing to follow directions. Most just ignored the fact that I was there and talked to their friends for the entire class period.

I attempted to teach them some vocal warm-ups. They had never done this before. A few polite people in the group started to participate, but the rebels vastly outnumbered them. Although some in the class made some initial weak attempts at cooperation, the sound was quickly extinguished. I gave up, handed out their music, and let them talk for the remaining ten minutes of class. The next day was worse.

After nearly twenty years of teaching, I had made a rookie mistake: I wanted them to like me. I lost control of that class for the entire year in the first five minutes by setting the wrong tone. I went to the principal who hired me to ask for help. He came in and sat in my room for every rehearsal for two weeks to restore order to my classroom. How embarrassing! Those students did accomplish a few things musically that year, but they never saw me as the authority figure in the classroom. That was a lesson hard learned, but one I'll never forget.

In the interests of sparing you some time and embarrassment, I'm going to tell you what to do on that first day so that the rest of your year is productive.

THE FIRST DAY OF SCHOOL

Some schools have a full schedule on the first day back to school in the fall. Ours has a short day where students go to each class but only for about eight minutes. That doesn't give me very much time to go over everything they need to know in order to succeed in my class, so I have to prioritize. Here are the items that I discuss with them, in order of importance:

1. The seating chart—where each student sits
2. Where they should put their non-class-related belongings
3. How the behavior plan and "checkbook" work
4. What I expect to accomplish by the end of the year
5. How my grading system works
6. The "handbook"

In eight minutes, all I really have time to do is tell the students where they sit. That issue really weighs most heavily on their minds; if they come back the next day and already know where to sit, they will probably be ready to listen to the rest of what you have in store for them.

The first day of school is your best opportunity to take control of your classroom. Arrive early and come prepared. When your students arrive, stand in the hallway just outside the door of your classroom. Greet each student as he or she arrives; tell them they may sit wherever they wish for the next minute and a half. Be welcoming but not overly friendly. Practice good posture and authority-figure facial expressions in the mirror before the first day. Nervous behavior like giggling and smiling will ruin you, especially if you are teaching middle school.

As soon as the bell rings, stand in front of the first chair in the first row and announce the name of the person who will occupy that seat on a permanent or at least semi-permanent basis. Continue to the next chair, and each consecutive chair, until all students are seated. In my experience, students are quiet the first day of school until they know what to expect, especially if they view the teacher as an authority figure. Use this to your advantage and get your students seated according to your plan as quickly as possible. When your students are where they are supposed to be, tell them to look and see exactly what row and seat they have been assigned to, and write it down if necessary. Let them know you expect to see them in exactly the same place the next day. If time allows, tell them where you would like them to store their belongings.

If I accomplish that within eight minutes, I'm very happy. If you have more than eight minutes on the first day, go ahead and proceed to the next step. If you're like me, however, you have to wait until the next day to proceed.

On the second day of school, after greeting students as they enter the room, I make sure that my class has mastered the skill I introduced the previous day by ensuring that everyone is in their assigned seats and that their belongings are in the appropriate place. In the past, when I had a full class period on the first day of school, I gave students applied practice on this skill by counting to ten, having them move to a different location, and then counting to ten again while they returned to their assigned seat.

Once students have learned the seating chart, you need to address the policies and procedures you have regarding the bathroom and drinks. Make it clear that you will not tolerate the interruption of your rehearsals and that students must follow your procedures in order to accomplish the goals you have set for them.

Now that they know where to sit and the protocol for leaving the room should the necessity arise, the next most important information for you to dispense is your behavior plan. This process has three steps. First, tell your class what you expect at each rehearsal. Have a poster listing the expectations you have in your checkbook and explain clearly what each one means. For instance, if I expect that students be prepared for class and in their seat when rehearsal begins, I explain that they need to have their music and a pencil in their lap and be in their seat when I begin warm-ups. If you teach orchestra, you probably want them to have their instrument and rosined bow ready and their music folder and a pencil on their stand. All other belongings should be somewhere else, such as under their seat.

Second, explain the consequences of not meeting these expectations. Show students your checkbook, explain clearly your procedure for marking infractions, and go over the consequences for each check they receive. I tell my students that if I call their name and point at the checkbook, they must come up to the front of the room without disrupting the rest of the rehearsal and put their initials in the appropriate box. I explain to them that they receive a detention for three checks during a one-week period.

Third, explain the rewards of good behavior and how and when a check can be eliminated. I tell students that they begin each week with a clean slate. Any student with fewer than two checks is eligible for the weekly drawing, and students who earn an "above and beyond" check may either erase a negative check or add an additional entry to the weekly prize drawing.

You may answer questions at this point, but if you teach middle school students, be aware that questions are their favorite tactic for avoiding your lesson plan. Be concise and let them know that everything you tell them is clearly explained in the handbook they will receive before they leave your classroom at the end of the period.

Next, give an overview of class activities for the year. Make it perfectly clear to your students that the focus of your class is performance and that their participation in concerts at your school is required (along with other performances you may also require). No exceptions. If your students are like mine, hands will immediately shoot into the air and questions will spill forth about hypothetical tragedies that might prevent attendance at concerts. Do not entertain these questions. Move on.

After you outline the required performances, you might also let them know about additional opportunities that are optional but encouraged. For me, this includes solo and ensemble contests and auditioning for district festivals. Our holiday mall performance is optional because the school provides no transportation to this event, but it is still well attended. The competition we attend at Six Flags is also optional because of the cost, but I encourage everyone to go and assure them that they will have enough opportunity to raise the money through fundraisers.

Lastly, as you cover the activities for the year, you will want to mention any other events that happen in your department. My music department takes a trip each year to Chicago to see a Broadway musical. This trip rewards the students for their hard work during the year. Personally, I prefer reward trips such as this to be musical in nature, but that's your decision. I think it's important to let students know what opportunities exist for careers in music, even if only a very few might ever reach that level. The National Association for Music Education (NAfME) National Standards 6 (listening to, analyzing, and describing music), 7 (evaluating music and music performances), and 8 (understanding relationships between music, the other arts, and disciplines outside the arts) are also addressed by taking trips such as this.

Recorded performances of music play an important part in meeting these standards, but live performances offer an entirely different experience. Students can see the actual people perform. For some students, this may be the first time they have an opportunity to see and hear a live concert or show. By exposing your classes to live performances, you give them the opportunity to compare live music with recordings, thus creating another avenue to explore when they write their critiques.

REWARD GOOD BEHAVIOR

If you mention that the end-of-the-year reward for good behavior is a trip to see a musical, you may not get the enthusiastic response you expect from your students. Some of them might not even know what a musical is. I tell them that we "will take a luxury charter bus—one with air conditioning and movies—to Chicago to see a Broadway musical." They don't hear much after I tell them about the luxury bus going to Chicago. They couldn't care less where it's going, particularly if it means they get to miss some classes the day of the trip.

Our trip to Chicago also gets lots of parents involved because we offer tickets to parents as well, and about 75 percent of all students going take at least one parent with them. Logistically, this is quite an undertaking, but here's how I do it: The first step is to find a show that is appropriate for our students and that runs late in the spring. The next step is to call the group sales office for the theater and order tickets. When I call Broadway in Chicago, I give them the closest estimate possible and the dates that would work for us. They send us an invoice, and we pay a first installment after collecting an initial payment from students and their parents.

Next, I call the charter bus services in our area, get quotes for the trip, and make sure that they can transport school students. Laws in different states vary on this. I choose the lowest quote, and they, too, send us an invoice. The total cost of the trip for students and parents is the cost of the bus divided by the number of riders plus the cost of the show ticket. We do not stop anywhere either before or after the show to eat. This is just an extra complication that I'm not willing to undertake. I tell the students to bring a sack lunch on the bus—but check with the bus company for their policies regarding food and drink first.

Closer to the actual day of the trip, I provide the theater with a final head count and make the final payment using funds collected, once again, from students and their parents. The trip is not required due to the expense but is well attended. Our Music Boosters help by covering the costs for students with financial difficulties. This is a little tricky, but I've found the best way to determine need is to check with the office to see who qualifies for free or reduced-price lunches. Sometimes, however, this is classified information and not available to you. When you send home information about the trip, make sure to let parents know that they can notify the office if financial difficulty would prevent their child from going on the trip and that the office keeps that information confidential.

The logistics of organizing a trip like this can be a little daunting but well worth the effort. If you know other teachers who have experience planning trips like this, it's a great idea to ask them exactly how it's done in your area.

THE HANDBOOK

Let's get back to the procedures of the first full day of class. The final item you need to cover is your grading system. This, of course, is all explained in the handbook you're about to distribute, but you need to tell your students. Some of them will never read that handbook. They even sign it, saying they've read it, but they haven't.

Pass out the handbooks to each person and give them a due date, which they should write in their planner, for returning the parent-signed agreement. Let them know that you will issue check marks for each day beyond the due date that it is returned and that, if after three days it still has not been returned, you will mail a copy home to their parents and issue a detention. (Remember? Three checks equal a detention.) Having the signed agreements in your hand is crucial if any arguments arise about whether someone knew about a procedure or concert. You can just pull out those students' sheets and show them that they signed this page saying that they read and understood all the information in the handbook. Voilà! You're covered.

Now you can send your precious pupils on to their next class, knowing that you've laid the groundwork for a fabulous year.

THE FIRST WEEK OF SCHOOL

Well, you survived the first full day of school, and your students have some idea of what to expect when they come into your room from now on. Now it's extremely important to follow through on every item to the letter of your law. Any bending of any one of your rules will be seen by your students as a sign of vulnerability and an opportunity to weaken your regime. Your class, after all, is not a democracy. It is a dictatorship.

Whatever categories you have for checks, as soon as your students come in on the second full day of class, you need to have your checkbook in hand and scrutinize the troops for any infringements. If they come in late, without a pass, it's a check. If they don't have a pencil on their stand, it's a check. If they're sitting with good posture in their chair, it's an above and beyond check (and sometimes a Jolly Rancher). Remember that rewarding good behavior is as important as correcting bad behavior.

I spend the majority of the first week of school enforcing my rules. If we get a little bit of music learned too, that's great, but it's not my first priority. If good behaviors are well established during that first week, learning music will be a breeze during subsequent weeks of school. With the incoming sixth graders or freshmen, I might even have them "practice" coming into the room, putting their belongings in the assigned place, getting instruments or music, sitting in their assigned chair (with good posture, of course), and placing a pencil on their stand. Then I do the reverse order to teach them the correct procedure for leaving my classroom, which includes sitting in their seats until the bell rings. They'll think it's childish, and they might giggle or even complain, but they'll know absolutely what you expect them to do every day.

Catch your students doing something good. Make a goal to give out at least as many "above and beyond" check marks as you do for the behaviors you're trying to correct. I give out "perfect posture" awards and "big mouth" awards (to students who actually open their mouths while singing). Be creative! Find ways to reward behaviors you want to reinforce. I just stop in the middle of a warm-up or rehearsal, walk over to a student who is sitting up straight, hand him or her a small certificate, and tell the class it's a "perfect posture" award. You can bet the rest of the class sits up straight immediately!

They can redeem these awards for small prizes, or you can just give out "above and beyond" checks. I find that, especially during the first week, it helps promote good behavior to physically hand out awards. When those behaviors start to wane, I start up again. The students never know when I might give them out.

In addition to rewarding individual students, I like to promote a "team" atmosphere by recognizing achievements of the class as a whole. If there are no check marks by anyone for an entire week, every student gets a reward, such as free time, students' choice music or activity, or a concert video. It drives me nuts when teachers give out whole-class punishments, because well-behaved students get punished for something someone else did, but whole-class rewards are great. Students start encouraging their classmates to work together, and when that happens, there's no limit to what your ensemble can do.

Also during that first week of school, you need to collect signed handbook agreements. I make this the first item of business once everyone is seated on the second day of class. I collect the agreements from those who brought them back and write down checks for those who didn't. On the fourth day of class, a detention notice is given to any student who has not returned the agreement. I make a list of the noncompliant students so that I can mail the handbooks home to their parents along with an explanation of why I mailed the handbook home and why their child received a detention.

By the fifth day of class, or the end of the first full week of school, your students know the routine, and you can start concentrating on your real mission—teaching music. Just keep in mind, especially if you teach junior high or middle school, that routine is essential to the success of your ensemble. Every day I do things in exactly this order:

1. Meet the students at or near the door to the classroom when they enter
2. Take attendance and make announcements

3. Warm up
4. Sight-sing (or sight-read)
5. Review the previous day's work
6. Work on new music
7. Play through at least one piece or section of music from beginning to end
8. Put instruments and music away and return to seats to wait for the dismissal bell to ring

When students know exactly what to expect every day, their behavior is better because they don't see openings to cause you to deviate from your plan. Remember—when you are disorganized, your students will seize the opportunity to throw your plans into the dumper. Of course, the opposite is also true. When you run your class like a well-oiled machine, the students know exactly what to do and when to do it, and mischief is less likely to happen.

THREE

Following Your Plan

DON'T GET LAZY!

It's easy, once your students have learned your routine, rules, and procedures, to fall into a nice, comfortable pattern and get lax on your classroom policies. Don't do it! It's kind of like dieting. People think the hard part is losing the weight. It's not. The maintenance is the hard part. If you start getting lazy about your eating habits, the weight comes back on. If you start getting lazy about your classroom management habits, poor behavior begins.

You'll be tempted to be less diligent about issuing check marks because things will run smoothly for a while. You'll start to let little things slide. You know how I know this? It's happened to me. At the beginning of the year, check marks fly. I don't let any infraction go by. As the weeks go by, students behave better, and fewer and fewer check marks get recorded. They start testing me, but now I'm out of practice when it comes to noticing infractions and recording them. Students start taking advantage, and little by little, the control I have in my classroom erodes. I have to start all over again writing check marks like crazy in order to regain control. Students become unhappy because I didn't consistently follow my own behavior plan.

For instance, I have a rule in my classroom about lip gloss. I don't want to see anyone applying lip gloss after the bell rings to start class. Period. No exceptions. Why no lip gloss? Because one girl will take out a tube of lip gloss, and every other girl's head in the class turns to see what brand and color it is—hence, the "no lip gloss" rule. For the first few weeks of school, I issue a check mark every single time I see a tube of lip gloss come out of someone's backpack. By the middle of September, when girls have learned not to take out their lip gloss in the middle of class and we're deep into the music during rehearsal, someone slips and pulls a tube of lip gloss out of her pocket. I'm in the middle of a rehearsal and I notice it, but I let it go by since it's been a long time since someone broke that rule. Can you guess what happens the next day? You're right. More lip gloss. The next day, nearly every girl is applying lip gloss during class, so I start issuing check marks again.

"But Mrs. Haugland, Ellen didn't get a check mark yesterday, and she had lip gloss." I wasn't being consistent and it wasn't fair. They were right. Slip-ups like this chip away at the authority you work so hard to establish at the beginning of the year.

I'm trying to save you time. Learn from my mistakes; don't repeat them. Don't ever let the little things slide, or they will become big, ugly, and bad problems that deter you from your path of providing high-quality music education to your students. Make sure that you continue to correct poor behavior, but also make sure that you continue to reward good behavior.

It's hard to be completely fair all the time. You might miss something someone does once in a while. Another student might complain that he or she got a check mark when so-and-so didn't, and so-and-so did or didn't do the same exact thing. Don't give in. After all, you probably have a much higher number of your students in your class than the average classroom teacher does. Tell these complainants that you did see their infraction, and that's why they're getting a check mark.

Although you won't be able to see every kid at every moment, I'm going to give you some ideas of what might be trouble indicators.

Watch for students who hide their faces behind music stands. Seems obvious, doesn't it? Some kids are really good at hiding, though. Who knows what they're doing back there? You sure don't. Some students frequently have library books (or other books or magazines) on their stands. It's not that I discourage kids from reading library books; I just don't allow it during a rehearsal. If I have a sectional scheduled, then a library book would be great if they're not playing, but I don't allow them during a regular rehearsal.

Keep track of students who disappear during class with an initial reasonable excuse like "My reed is broken" or "I need to blow my nose." (Tip: If a student needs a tissue, I have them sniff for me. Sounds ridiculous, doesn't it? Well, I can tell from the sound of the sniff if they really need a tissue or if they're just looking for an excuse to get out of rehearsal.) Some kids specialize in such excuses to go hang out in the instrument storage room and hope you're so involved in the rehearsal that you won't notice they're gone the entire class period. Yes, this has happened to me.

I had a girl tell me she needed her rosin. I didn't notice that she never returned to the cello section until the end of class, when I saw her books still sitting under her chair. When she came to retrieve her books, I asked her where she'd been, and she said she was doing homework in the instrument storage room. I hope that's all she was doing in there. Pay attention to who's leaving, the reason why, and the length of time he or she is gone. If you let someone sneak out just once, you'll have an instant reputation as the teacher anyone can sneak out on.

You will have students who fake playing or singing. This is a really tough one to spot but very important. Though not necessarily a behavior problem, it's a sign that they might need extra help. If they don't get the extra help they need, they'll either become a behavior problem or drop out of your program. Once students start falling behind in skills, they get frustrated, lose self-confidence, and stop enjoying playing or singing. You need to determine the reason for students' habitual silence. It might be because they really don't want to be there, or it might be because they really don't understand how to play or sing. Pull these students aside privately and ask them. They'll probably tell you and be grateful for the help if they need it.

I'll never forget when my own daughter came home one day with the revelation that "orchestra is so much more fun when you can play the music!" I think it's safe to say that the opposite is also true—that is to say, "orchestra (or band or chorus) is not any fun at all if you can't play the music." If you have students who pretend to play, do all you can to get them extra help, and talk to their parents about making sure they're getting adequate practice time at home. If you don't, they'll be gone before you know it.

Consistency is key. Even if you're not new in your position, the behavior plan described above can work for you. Once your students realize that you're serious about what you do, they will accept the system. They may not necessarily like it, but that's okay. You're not there to be their friend; you're there to be their teacher. That doesn't mean that you have to be stern or humorless; it just means you need to be the figure of authority in your classroom. Even though they may not realize this until years after they have left your classroom, your students will ultimately respect you more for managing the class well and giving them a high-quality education.

REEVALUATE YOUR PLAN

I've spent most of my career teaching in rural schools in which the population of students is lower than that of many city schools and less culturally diverse. Where you teach may be much different. I believe this behavior plan will work in any classroom, but it may need to be tailored to fit your specific needs. For instance, the categories on my checklist work for me, and they might be a good place to start, but you may need to add to the list or change some of the items to make your classroom run efficiently.

After a few weeks, sit down and think about how things are going. What's happening in your classroom that you really like? Are there areas for improvement? How can you modify your plan to increase efficiency? If you know you have an aspect of your system that you'd like to improve but you're not sure what works, I suggest that you talk to some colleagues.

During your planning period, walk down the hall and notice what classes seem to be running smoothly. Ask your students; they can tell you who the best teachers are and why. Go talk to those teachers and find out what works for them. Good teachers love to share their ideas, so ask away. Again, their ideas may not work in your classroom exactly, but they might with some adaptation.

As teachers of performance-based classes, our class sizes are larger than regular classes and our rooms are desk-free. Sometimes, even with adaptations, what works in other classrooms in the building won't quite work for us. Going to other districts to observe teachers you respect is another fantastic way to learn techniques for classroom management.

Sometimes observing other teachers can also give you good examples of what not to do. In one of the schools where I worked, we were required to go do observations out of district at least twice a year. I went to a neighboring district to watch a teacher whom I knew was struggling, and it was easy to see why. While he was prepared for his classes and seemed to have a good management system in place, he paused too long between activities. Every time he finished rehearsing a piece of music, he sat silent or shuffled papers around for what seemed like an eternity before he started something else. The kids would start talking to each other and it took several minutes to get their attention back. Watching him made me painfully aware that I did the same thing quite often. I would get frustrated every time I lost the attention of my class, but after observing this teacher, it became crystal clear why it happened and I immediately corrected myself.

It doesn't hurt to videotape your rehearsals either. I can't stand watching myself, but it's a great way to catch yourself doing things you never imagined you were doing—such as saying "um" or "okay" a million times in a half hour, for instance. A director I worked with said "okay" almost every fifth word. His students kept tally marks counting how many "okays" he said during a rehearsal. Do you think they were paying any attention to any of his directions? Probably not. He didn't realize he was doing this until he watched a videotape of one of his rehearsals.

During professional conferences, seek out educators in your discipline. Find out what works and doesn't work for them. Keep asking and keep fine-tuning until you get your classroom working at an optimum performance level. Clean house—throw out the ideas that don't work and replace them with ideas that do work. Use caution, though. If you change too many pieces of your plan too often, it's the same as having no plan at all.

Give any potential changes serious consideration. Are they important enough to be added midstream, or could they wait until the next school year? If you decide to implement a change, you need to change your handbook, and that requires notifying the administration and the parents. They must sign off on the new policies, just as they did when they originally signed the page that said they read and understood everything in the handbook. Ask yourself if you really need to implement a change or if better enforcement of one part of your existing plan would improve your situation.

One year I considered making a change to my behavior checklist to include a category for remembering a pencil every day. When I thought about it, though, I already had that category. It's called "being prepared for class." I reminded the students that this particular category meant having the proper materials, including a pencil, when they came to my classroom, and that they would receive a check mark if they didn't have that pencil. They started bringing pencils. Perhaps you have a similar situation and part of your policy already covers what you need to address.

When considering a change to your plan, you also need to decide if a specific student or group of students is driving your decision, or if the change would benefit the class as a whole. If it's the former, perhaps you can find a better way to deal with an isolated person or group.

The first time I used the behavior plan, I had a student who really didn't like me at all. I know why she didn't like me, and it had nothing to do with my class. Her bad attitude was like a cancer in my classroom. No matter where I moved her, her nastiness spread to other students sitting next to her. I considered adding a category for attitude, but when you're dealing with middle school students, that's not very realistic. A better solution was to sit down with her, one on one, and also to inform her parents of the situation. She was never really happy in my class, but she stopped being a behavior problem.

As you're working with your plan for the first year or two, be sure to jot down new ideas when you come across them—and don't forget where you put your list. Perhaps your class runs well enough to leave your plan in place for the remainder of the current school year or semester, but you might want to make some adjustments for the following year. The longer you work with your plan, the better you'll know what to keep and what needs to go.

NETWORK

Once you develop a system that facilitates productive rehearsals of your ensemble, share what you're doing. Go to district and state conferences. Be active in the meetings and sessions you have with other educators in your field. Find out what they're doing in their schools. Whatever you do, do not isolate yourself in your own little corner of the world. Music education is an endangered curriculum, after all. The more programs that we have working effectively across the country, the more likely we are to convince administrators that music is an essential part of a child's overall education. It's vital that music educators network with each other and share good ideas.

Whether you're fighting to save your own program or trying to start a new one, it helps to know what's going on in surrounding schools as well as across the country. How does the fine arts curriculum in your school compare to similar districts? Most boards of education want their district to compare favorably in terms of enrollment, course offerings, and opportunities for students. They also want to know that the programs in their district enable students to perform better on standardized tests and college entrance exams. Working with other area directors helps you stay abreast of this type of information.

When I started up an orchestra program at the elementary school where I used to work, I had other area orchestra directors to thank, in large part. They brainstormed with me and helped me prepare a presentation for the board of education. Some of them even came to the board meeting and answered questions that the board members had regarding the logistics of adding a new program to the curriculum. I couldn't have gotten that program off the ground without the assistance I received from those other directors.

Since the first draft of this book, networking through the use of social media has exploded and the professional network that I've developed through Facebook and Twitter has become an essential lifeline. I can get an almost immediate answer to any question I have on any aspect of music education.

On Facebook, search for the group simply titled "Music Teachers." Teachers post and discuss topics immediately relevant to their classrooms on a daily basis. A testament to the power of social networking, over two thousand teachers joined this group in just a couple of months. Groups and informational pages are also available for just about every faction and methodology known to music education: Orff, Kodaly, ACDA (American Choral Directors Association), NAfME, and so on. The advantage of participating in Facebook groups is that the posts can foster lengthy discussions in more of a bulletin-board format—that is to say, the responses to the initial posts remain connected and easily visible and easy to read.

I also have a large professional network on Twitter and find it to be more immediate and concise. The rapid newsfeed pace on Twitter means that you sometimes have to sift through a lot of tweets to glean knowledge and information, depending on how many people you follow. However, I often find faster answers to my questions on Twitter because of the size of my network. Music education "tweet chats" on various topics are also available on a regularly scheduled basis. Try searching hashtags such as #musiced and #musedchat.

Another benefit of Twitter is the global nature of the beast. Facebook is also global, but it seems to me that music educators worldwide participate more on Twitter than on Facebook. If you're a night owl, someone on the other side of the planet may have an answer for you, or you might find a lively discussion in the wee hours when everyone stateside is asleep and, as a side benefit, you might gain a new perspective that previously escaped you.

When posting on Facebook, Twitter, Scoop, Pinterest, or any other site that crops up in the future, here are a few things to keep in mind:

- Keep your posts relevant.
- Be as succinct and eloquent as you are able to be.
- Say something worth retweeting (or reposting). This will grow your network.
- Be yourself.
- Shorten links if you are posting articles, videos, and so forth.
- Use hashtags to help others find you.
- Join and participate in discussion groups.
- Use good "netiquette." Don't type in all caps. Be polite. Don't post things you wouldn't want a future employer to see. In other words, use good common sense and remember that what you put out there stays forever.

In order to build your network, you'll have to find people to follow. Use the search boxes on the various sites and look for people who share your interests. Read their tweets or postings and see if they're worth your time. If you find someone interesting, look at who they follow for more leads. Mention them by name in your posts by typing "@" in front of their handle and both they and their followers will notice you. You follow, they follow back, and before you know it, you have a network.

Conferences become much more interesting when you have a professional network because you will get to meet the real-life people with whom you've conversed online, and the bonds of social media become even more powerful. If you're job hunting or looking for support, you know you have colleagues across the country, and sometimes all over the world, who can help you. All of this should be part of the plan you have for your classroom and for your career.

Will your plan work forever? Probably not. Your population of students changes. Times change. Educational philosophy changes. Technology changes. Don't be too rigid in your thinking or you'll be left behind—and so will your students.

FOUR

Creating a Team

An ensemble that feels like a team and works together performs better than one that doesn't. When you see or listen to a group that has this team spirit, you immediately recognize it in the energy of the performance. Sometimes, in schools with many socioeconomic levels or culturally diverse populations of students, getting students to come together and work as a team is one of the most difficult parts of managing a classroom that you can tackle.

Some books contain ideas for building teams with some fun ideas to try (see resources in appendix E). For instance, one of my favorite team-building games is "inner circle and outer circle." Before you start, make up a list of ten or so age-appropriate questions like "What's your favorite band?" or "Who do you think was the best president and why?" Divide your class into two groups; have one group form an inner circle and the other group form an outer circle around the inner circle. Have the students face each other and ask the first question. Give them a minute to discuss their answers, and then tell one of the groups to move a certain number of steps in either direction so they face a new partner. Ask another question. Repeat until all of the questions are ask or until you run out of time. Some of the kids may have never talked to one another, and this game gives them a little bit of insight into commonalities they may not have known about previously. Getting the students to discover ways they're alike rather than ways they're different is the key to creating a team atmosphere.

I have found one of the easiest ways to build a team is to simply work together toward a common goal. Some of our team-building activities include the following:

1. Competing in music festivals
2. Working together on fundraisers

3. Performing in the community
4. Creating "pride wear"
5. Organizing community service projects

COMPETING IN MUSIC FESTIVALS

You likely have a different goal in your school, but the ultimate goal at the end of each school year with my ensembles is to compete at the festival at Six Flags. We bring back a big trophy every year. Everyone who participated the previous year wants to go back and improve their excellent performances, and those who haven't gone yet can't wait to get their hands on a trophy themselves.

Music festivals offer a great opportunity to prepare your ensemble for a performance that has the critique of an expert (other than you). You could compete against other ensembles, perform for an adjudicator who gives a written or taped critique, or even do a clinic with your group. The first time I took my choirs to a festival, we competed for "ratings only," which meant that the judges taped their comments during a performance and gave us a point-based rating, but we did not compete with other schools. For their first time out, I thought that students might be so disappointed if they placed behind other ensembles that it would negatively affect morale. However, when I received the rating sheets that included the scores for all of the choirs participating, I learned that not only would we have placed first in our division but we also had the second-highest score of all of the choirs.

We entered the competition the next year and every year since. We haven't always placed first, but the kids always try their hardest; they're winners in my heart and they know it. Singing or playing in a festival or competition where students know they're being graded is a totally different experience from performing for their families and friends. It's not enough that you and their parents tell them they're wonderful all year long. It's an extra reward to receive praise from a stranger whom they know is a specialist. Working together all year with the final goal—the best possible performance at festival—creates an incredibly strong sense of team, and it carries forward from year to year.

WORKING TOGETHER ON FUNDRAISERS

Sometimes you need to raise funds in order to be able to go to those festivals. Sometimes you must raise funds for other things, like reward trips, uniforms, music stands, or even music. Fundraising is a necessity in almost every school district. If you do it right, it can also be a bonding experience for your group because they all work together to help the ensemble.

The trip to the festival at Six Flags is expensive for our families. It costs about $75 per student, and this includes the charter buses, entrance fees, and meals. I want every student to be able to go, regardless of the cost, so I offer several opportunities for the students to fundraise their way there. Like most schools districts, we have students from extremely affluent families, very poor families, and everywhere in between. When we work together toward a common goal, there are no socioeconomic lines; there is just the team. Everyone works together so everyone can go to Six Flags to compete.

Our rehearsals throughout the entire school year constitute the training for this final event. When students understand this, they have the motivation to work together at each and every rehearsal. All students know that we depend on every member for each performance and contest. If any team member was not able to participate in the final competition due to financial concerns, the entire team would suffer. Given that knowledge, the students work hard on all of the fundraising projects to make sure that the entire team is able to go to Six Flags.

Some students have parents who would prefer that their children not participate in fundraisers. They worry about their kids going to strangers' houses to sell things (even though we expressly direct them not to do this), or they might hesitate to approach friends and family, since almost every activity in which their child participates requires fundraising. This is why I work hard to find new and creative ways to raise money that don't involve selling wrapping paper or candy. Those things are fine and they're easy, but so many different groups do them that the profits tend to diminish.

If parents prefer to pay fees themselves, that's fine, but I explain to them in a meeting at the beginning of the year how our fundraising events bring the students together as a team. I also ask for ideas about ways to earn money. I want them to know that most of the students work so hard at fundraising that we have enough for everyone to be able to go on the trip, regardless of their ability to pay. We may even have funds to pay for both concert shirts and team T-shirts for everyone. It's very important that parents know exactly how the money earned is spent. They're far more likely to be supportive if they are well informed.

The fundraising puts all students on a level playing field. All are encouraged to participate. We rehearse as a team, we get to the performance as a team, and we perform as a team.

The biggest fundraiser that we hold requires participation of all of my students. We hold what we call a "Ladies' Day" vendor and crafter fair. We pamper women and give local merchants, service providers, and crafters an opportunity to showcase their businesses. This event would not work if we didn't have every student working together to pull it off.

Ladies' Day is held in the school gym on the first Sunday in March from one to four in the afternoon. During the weeks prior to that Sunday, students visit local businesses to sell booth space for $30 for a ten-by-ten-foot area in the gym. Vendors must bring their own tables and chairs. We invite nail technicians and massage therapists to come as well. We don't charge them for booth space but ask that they provide their services free of charge to our guests. They use this opportunity to hand out business cards to build their clientele. Students sell tickets to the event for $5 each. This includes admission to the craft fair, free manicures and massages, cookies, and flavored coffees. For the first one hundred guests, we also have travel coffee mugs that were custom printed with our Cardinal Chorus logo. We pay for the mugs with funds from the advance ticket sales.

We promote the event by going on local television news and radio morning shows. I take the coffee mug with me, along with some extra tickets to give away. We take group pictures and submit them to the local papers for publicity as well. Flyers are printed and hung on every available bulletin board locally and in neighboring communities. The vendors are much more enthusiastic about buying booth space if they understand how well we promote the event. They want to make sure they will have customers.

Students bring home-baked cookies the day before the event, and I buy coffee and creamers in several different flavors (both regular and decaf, of course). We also get good disposable coffee cups with lids, like they have in coffee shops, which are easier for the guests to carry around while they shop. Parents bring in nice trays for the cookie table and we decorate it with pretty tablecloths and flowers.

The actual day of the event, students are assigned shifts to help vendors unload and set up, make and serve coffee and cookies, babysit children of our customers, and, of course, clean up afterward. Everyone works together to make the day a successful event, and we all share in the reward of a lower out-of-pocket cost for our trip. We do other fundraisers as well (we even sell wrapping paper), but the Ladies' Day event does more to get the kids working together than any of the others.

I've worked in a district where the classroom budget is nearly limitless, and I've worked in a district where the total yearly budget for instrumental music was $800. If your budget is huge, then maybe you don't need to do as much fundraising. In my experience, though, students have more ownership of the program if they have the opportunity to contribute not only with their musicianship but also with service to the organization.

DISADVANTAGED STUDENTS

If you teach instrumental music, you know that band and orchestra students have other financial obligations to consider in addition to trip costs.

Instrument costs can be prohibitive for many families. But every student should have the opportunity to learn to play a musical instrument. How do you make sure they all have access to an instrument?

Our school owns several instruments. A portion of our fundraising each year goes toward the purchase of at least one new instrument, and part of our small classroom budget is designated for maintenance of those school-owned instruments. When we loan a student a school instrument, we have the family sign a contract agreeing to properly care for the borrowed instrument.

Some instruments have additional costs associated with them, so you need to consider the family's ability to pay for these expenditures. For instance, reed instrument players obviously need reeds, and some of them are much more expensive than others. String instruments periodically need strings, and cello strings are much more expensive than violin strings (although they're also less likely to break).

Think about all of the costs associated with each instrument (cork grease, valve oil, cleaning swabs, rosin, and so on), and consider whether or not your student's family can afford those extras, or if your classroom budget can provide them.

Our community is fortunate to have a music store that rents instruments at a greatly reduced cost or even at no charge if the music director refers the family. In our community, the owner of the store is one of the biggest advocates for music education, and he started the program to help families struggling financially. He doesn't publicize what he calls "music for all" but lets area directors know that they can refer families for instruments at reduced or free rental. If we know a child is on the free or reduced-price lunch program at school, that automatically qualifies them; if we are aware of other circumstances, we can refer them as well.

You might want to check with your local dealers to see if they offer a program like this one. Local community service organizations, your Music Booster organizations, and even foundations such as VH1's Save the Music are resources you can look into to help disadvantaged students who want to learn to play an instrument. Your team should be dressed uniformly with properly working, high-quality instruments, and every student in your school should have an equal opportunity to be a part of that team. Sometimes it just requires a little extra resourcefulness on your part to make that happen.

PERFORMING IN THE COMMUNITY

Performing often gives ensembles a sense of pride. I mentioned in chapter 1 that we hold holiday performances at a local mall every year. I always look for performance venues for our groups outside of our school gym. The holidays are the perfect time to showcase your ensemble. Perhaps your local merchants have special open houses or shopping nights, and they might like some music outside their store. Call and ask them.

Our town has a holiday shopping kickoff night in November that they call "Miracle on 2nd Street." All the local merchants stay open late; the event has horse-drawn carriage rides, hot chocolate, and goodies, and almost every store has musicians. I have the kids form small ensembles, trios and quartets, and they rotate between stores for an hour or so during that night.

Keep your eyes open for opportunities to make your ensemble more visible. Local clubs like the Kiwanis and Rotary clubs often look for entertainment for their meetings. Perhaps your local chamber of commerce has a luncheon or other function where your students could play or sing. Do you have a VA hospital or senior center near you? If you just sit and think about it, you can probably come up with lots of ideas.

Students get excited to have audiences beyond their family and friends, and they enjoy performing in different locations. Of course, when they perform for the public, they want to do their absolute best, and they work together even more than they do for our regular school performances. Scheduling a variety of community performances leading up to the final competition keeps that spirit alive throughout the course of the year.

CREATING PRIDE WEAR

We have our concert performance T-shirts that we wear at formal and semi-formal performances, but we also have "pride wear." When the students perform in regular concerts, contests, and festivals, they wear their concert dress. For less formal events, though, students wear pride-wear T-shirts and blue jeans. I do specify blue jeans—not black, not gray, but blue jeans. Even though the look is more casual, it should still be uniform. Our T-shirts are designed by one of our students at the beginning of the school year. All students who wish to submit a design have an opportunity to do so, and we take a blind vote for the one that will represent our group. I have also, in the past, had a panel of teachers choose the design to prevent it from being a popularity contest.

Designs must be done in heavy black ink on unlined white paper. We've had T-shirts that included both front and back artwork, and some that had front-only or back-only artwork. Once the design is chosen, I fax it to area screen printers for quotes. Some years we have everyone with the same color T-shirt, while in other years we've randomly assigned a rainbow of colors. Students hand in the size T-shirt they want, and I place orders accordingly. Depending on the size of the group, I order between two and five extra shirts in each size for students who come into the district later and for those who inevitably lose or damage their shirts. Our local sporting goods store has always given us the lowest price per shirt (usually $7 or less); it's easy to drop off the artwork and pick up the shirts, and I like giving the local merchants our business.

I specify that the school will pay for the students' first concert T-shirt and pride-wear T-shirt, but if the shirt is lost or damaged, the student must pay for a replacement. We pay for these shirts out of our fundraising activity fund, but you have other options. Music Boosters might help with this, you might charge a class fee to cover the shirts, or you might have the students bring in money to cover the cost. The latter is my least favorite option because families never cooperate 100 percent when it comes to sending in money.

The students wear these peer-designed T-shirts for casual events such as the mall performances and school assemblies, and also at the Six Flags theme park once the contest part of the day is over. They can be easily identified as part of our group this way and, more importantly, they show their pride in being part of our group. I see the shirts very frequently during regular school days because most of the students are proud to wear their shirts at school.

COMMUNITY SERVICE

The final team-building idea I want to share with you is that of community service. Many schools now make community service part of their graduation requirements. These schools recognize that community service fosters an awareness and understanding of social and civic responsibility and gives students pride in the contributions they can make by supporting and strengthening their communities.

When we choose a charity to benefit, I like to have someone from that particular organization come speak to the students about the type of service they provide. For the last three years, we have raised funds for a local food pantry. I have each of my classes create their own fundraiser, and I give a donut party on the morning before our winter break to the class that raises the most funds.

Our most successful community service venture involved voting for a teacher to sing a solo at our holiday concert. My students approached the teachers of their other classes and asked if they'd be willing to participate. Students told teachers they would collect votes in the form of quarters for a very worthy cause. If a particular teacher received the most votes, they would sing a four-bar solo with the choir at the holiday concert—just the first phrase of the chorus of one of the songs. We decorated coffee cans and placed them on the desks of the willing candidates. Students voted by putting a quarter in the can of their favorite would-be soloist.

Last year, the sixth-grade team of teachers had quite a rivalry and it sparked a voting frenzy. The week before voting ended, each teacher went down the halls collecting votes for the other candidates so that he or she wouldn't win. The chosen soloist who received the most quarters was a young teacher named Mr. Vogel. The students just loved him, and they voted like crazy. They didn't just put quarters in his can; they stuffed wads of green paper money in it.

Not only were the chorus students extra excited about that holiday concert, but we also recorded our highest audience attendance that year because so many non-chorus students and their parents showed up to see Mr. Vogel sing. He did a darned nice job, too. I was impressed!

Other very profitable events included holding silent auctions at our concerts, having bake sales during student lunch hour, and delivering marshmallow crispy treats in what is now our annual Christmas Crispy sale. For $1, staff and students can send a crispy treat to another student or staff member. We set up a table in the lunchroom where other students, staff members, and employees purchase a crispy treat, which is delivered the week before winter break. People purchasing the crispy treats can write a gift card attached to the cookie before delivery.

The day before the actual delivery, my students bring in pans of crispy treats, which they have prepared at home the night before. They are given recipes and instructed to press them into nine-by-thirteen-inch pans and are also given instructions on how to cut them so that everyone gets the same size cookie. We bag the cookies, attach the gift tags, and deliver them to the addressees the morning before winter break.

Your students can come up with endless ideas to raise funds, or they can volunteer time at local agencies. The idea, though, is to work together to formulate and carry out a plan. Pride in their accomplishment as a result of their team effort goes a long way toward increasing cohesiveness as an ensemble. Besides that, it's a nice thing to do.

COMMUNICATION

The team you create needs to consist of not only you and your students but also the parents of your students and the administration of the school. Communication is the key. When it comes to parents, send detailed notes or newsletters home about upcoming concerts, projects, fundraisers, and trips. Since middle and high school students are not particularly adept at delivering notes to their parents, it's helpful to have e-mail groups set up so you can quickly and easily send these notices directly to the parents. Sending a copy to your administrators is also necessary.

Almost all schools ask for e-mail addresses at registration, and your information technology specialist (if you have one) should be able to help you set up an e-mail group with the e-mail addresses of your students' parents. If that doesn't happen, you can add a section to your handbook and ask for that information on the page that they sign and return. Keep in mind that not every house has access to e-mail and also that people who do have access don't always read their e-mail. It's not a foolproof method of getting information to everyone, but if you send both paper copies and e-mail, you reach most of them.

Our school district has just instituted an automatic phone calling system. You can use this in the same way as e-mail, and in our district, many more homes have telephones than computers. People also tend to check their phone messages more often than they check their e-mail, so this is a great option if you have access to a similar system.

Most school districts now have individual websites for teachers. Make good use of yours! Update your page often with pictures of what you're doing in class (be sure to check about parental permission for photos of students and their work), concert dates, special activities, fundraising, and so on. It's often much easier for parents to look for information on your website than it is to search for an old e-mail that you might have sent, or the handbook that you sent home at the beginning of the year. Make all that information available with a few clicks of their mouse.

During the first few weeks of school, let all the parents know about the importance of attending Music Boosters meetings, and perhaps organize a committee of parents to help you with different events throughout the year. The more parents you involve, the more support you build for your program and the stronger your team is.

I've been involved with several different Music Boosters organizations over the years, and I've seen well-organized thriving groups and ones that were actually detrimental to the health of the school music program. As the music director, you need to be actively involved. Your job is to educate these parents, most of whom have the best of intentions, on how to be advocates for music education in your school. A large part of what the boosters do is fundraising, and that is certainly necessary, but if you're the only one in town yelling about how important music education is, not many people hear the message.

If you're in a new position and a Music Boosters organization already exists, you need to do more listening than talking at the first few meetings to get an idea of what their role has been in the past. The last parent group I worked with had really only concentrated on fundraising. That was all they knew and all they talked about at meetings. I gradually and gently started adding advocacy topics to the agendas at the meetings, and little by little their focus shifted. They still continued to raise funds, but with more of a purpose.

NAfME has some great publications (see appendix E) that are helpful when you're looking for information to pass along to the group that's supporting you and your program. The Internet has many sites devoted to advocacy in music education, and VH1 has some great material too (see appendix E).

The parents of your students should be just as much a part of your team as are their kids. As I will discuss in more detail later, it's absolutely vital that you organize a group that is ready at any time to come to the defense of the music program in your school. Do not wait until you need them, because by then it may be too late.

FIVE

Projects, Process, and Purpose

Classroom management is a huge umbrella that covers so much more than just behavioral and organizational issues. Part of managing your classroom is preparing and planning your curriculum. You probably have great ideas about what you want to teach, but have you mapped out when and how those lessons will happen throughout the year? Being a well-organized teacher with thoughtfully prepared lesson plans conveys to your students that the course you teach is serious business. Helping students make connections between the music they play and the world around them is an important part of your job, and planning class projects makes that happen.

The first five content standards from the National Association for Music Education (NAfME) are performance related and are well covered by your curriculum, since you teach a performance-based class. However, your class must still address National Standards 6–9. These standards include listening to, analyzing, and describing music (Standard 6); evaluating music and music performances (Standard 7); understanding relationships between music, the other arts, and disciplines outside the arts (Standard 8); and understanding music in relation to history and culture (Standard 9). You can enrich your students' knowledge of the music they play or sing and the different cultures represented by that music.

At the time that this edition is being written, the National Standards are being revised by the National Coalition for Core Arts Standards (NCCAS) and are not yet available. Additionally, the Common Core standards for English language arts and mathematics are being implemented across the United States. At first glance, Common Core appears to have nothing to do with music education, but in fact the implications for music education are many and I will discuss this more at the end of this chapter.

One big benefit of using projects to enhance your curriculum is that your students have much more interest in the music they practice on a daily basis and become more engaged in their daily rehearsals. The other benefit is that students, parents, administrators, and other faculty members view your class as being more academic in nature if you require your kids to learn more about the music they perform. If you work with other teachers on cross-curricular units, you might find that they think of you as a regular faculty member and not just as a "special." You build more support for your program, and that's always a good thing.

Integrated curriculum has been a topic of some discussion over the last several years. Whether it's called integrated curriculum or interdisciplinary study, the idea is that children are taught in a way that cuts across departmentalized subject lines. An emphasis on student projects using sources beyond textbooks is used to help students discover relationships between different aspects of a particular topic. Frequently, when an integrated curriculum is taught, students work in cooperative groups, and teachers might even team-teach. If you're open to the idea of teaching this way, you might find your own creativity ignited, and your job might become significantly more interesting and maybe even more fun!

When you say you're willing to integrate your curriculum, you have to use some caution because core subject area teachers often think that means you'll teach your kids a song about pollution if they do a unit on the environment. This helps them out somewhat, but it does next to nothing to advance your curriculum, and it certainly doesn't address the NAfME content standards.

However, if you can show that you integrate other subject areas (reading, writing, math, social studies) into your teaching, then you simultaneously help students, please administrators, and enhance your program. My students complete four projects a year—one for each quarter. When planning these assignments, you need to keep a few things in mind.

These projects should relate to the music you're performing in order to help students better understand what they play. Making connections for students is crucial. Finding links between the music they're playing and familiar history gives them a better understanding of the music.

Let's say your group is playing a minuet; wouldn't students have a better concept of the style if they were familiar with the period of history during which this dance was popular? Have them look at costumes from that era and imagine themselves dancing in them. Women had tight corsets and big, wired undergarments to hold their skirts far away from their bodies. Men wore silk stockings and high ruffled collars. Would they dance at a quick or slow tempo when they're worried about their powdered wigs falling off? Make a timeline showing what was happening in the United States during this period. Who would have been president? George Washington? And yes, he did wear a powdered wig! That's familiar to your students; they probably learned that in first grade.

Minuets were written during the baroque era. Do your students know what baroque instruments were like? Do they know that cellists had no endpins to help them hold their cellos off the floor? Explaining the limitations of the period instruments helps create an understanding of the composer's stylistic ideas. You could show a video of a baroque orchestra playing on period instruments and really illustrate what you're talking about.

Another consideration when planning a project is the variety of learning styles among your students. Learning styles are simply different approaches or ways of learning. Gardner's multiple intelligences theory is one model of learning styles. Gardner theorizes that we don't have one intelligence but rather several different intelligences. Each of us possesses all of these intelligences, but we all have strengths in different areas that affect the way we learn. Gardner's seven core intelligences are as follows: bodily and kinesthetic, linguistic, logical and mathematical, spatial, interpersonal, intrapersonal, and . . . musical!

If, for instance, a student has a stronger bodily and kinesthetic intelligence, he or she could learn better through methods of teaching compatible with that learning style. Using Curwen hand signs while singing, for example, might help that student understand intervallic relationships better because he or she is using motion to learn. Students with mathematical and logical strength look for patterns to help them learn. Someone who has a strong linguistic intelligence is particularly sensitive to the spoken or written word. Spatial learners learn by visually studying the placement of notes on a staff. Interpersonal strengths allow people to learn better by working in small groups, while intrapersonal learners would rather work by themselves. Musical learners learn best while playing, singing, or listening to music.

Gardner's multiple intelligences theory is one example of a learning-style model, but certainly not the only one. Models by Rita and Kenneth Dunn, David Kolb, Richard Felder, and Linda Silverman are also quite popular. The bottom line is that different kids learn best in different ways. Think about giving them a choice of several different ways to complete a project. If you teach in only one way, you won't get through to all of your students. If you only give written assignments or tests, some of your students won't understand the connection you're trying to make for them. I'll go into different options for projects in more depth in a minute.

When assigning projects, you need to post them the same way other teachers do. If your school's website has a homework page, learn how to use it. I made a big mistake the first time I gave out an assignment. I expected the students to write it in their planners and get it done on time without letting their parents know they had an assignment from me with a deadline. What I didn't realize was that our school has a homework hotline and a website for homework so parents can check to make sure that their child is doing what he or she is supposed to do. Once I posted my assignments on the hotline, it was amazing how many more were turned in on time.

Students who have had private instruction before coming to your class might be able to use these projects as a way to use their advanced abilities. Since the explosion of Suzuki instruction across the country, music educators have struggled with the question of what to do with students who have had years of instruction before enrolling in public school music programs. Cross-curricular projects put everyone on a level playing field. Every student can work at his or her own level and use their individual strengths.

Appendix C has examples of projects to give you an idea of the creativity you can unleash when creating these assignments. Students who are not necessarily your finest musicians may really find their chance to shine.

It's my personal opinion that students practice harder on music they understand or to which they have made a cognitive connection. They also use better phrasing and play or sing with more passion. The connections you make between the music and other areas of knowledge help you create more well-rounded musicians and appreciators of music.

The year 2006 was the 250th anniversary of Mozart's birth. I programmed several pieces from different stages of Mozart's life for our spring concert. As an introduction, we watched a video about Mozart, during which the students were encouraged to take notes for a quiz to follow. I allowed them to use their notes and the quiz was very easy, but the kids paid a lot more attention to the information when they had to take notes for a quiz. Following this introduction to Mozart, we discussed the periods during which he wrote the music we would perform. We talked about what he might have been feeling at that time of his life and how the music might reflect those feelings. We also sang or played through certain passages that might have highlighted our discussion. The difference in their musicality once they had a deeper understanding of the composer was incredible.

Then I gave them a choice of ways they could complete their project, trying to keep Gardner's theory of multiple intelligences in mind. Some students preferred to work alone and not to get up in front of the class to present their work. The best choice for them was to write an essay giving an overview of Mozart's life. I selected a particularly shining example of the essays to be used as an insert in our concert program.

Other students enjoyed working in groups and performing. They preferred to write a short skit in which Mozart was being interviewed about his life. Some of the more technically advanced students chose to perform a work by Mozart and take questions from the rest of the class about the specific piece being played.

Some students excelled in spatial reasoning and chose to make a timeline or mobile of the events in Mozart's life that influenced his music. I hung these in the performance area on the night of our concert, but I also gave the students the option of presenting them to the class.

In my experience, when given choices that appeal to their areas of strength, students get much more excited about working on the project, and their work is very thorough and sometimes downright amazing.

Another assignment that I give during the year is to write program notes for our performances. Some care has to be used when doing this, though, because not every piece of music has history that can be researched by the student. When you're performing newly composed pieces, often there is little to no information available about either the composer or the music. However, if the composition is an arrangement of a folk song, or even just contains fragments of folk music, those can be researched quite well, and a discussion of how the old music is used in the new work can be written.

If your ensembles are performing new music, you could have them write more analytical essays than historical essays. Students can talk about the form of the piece, or even editorialize about the piece. Without a doubt, your students have opinions about the music they're performing. Let them be critics and constructively communicate their feelings in an essay.

One other project I assign is to specifically address NAfME Standard 9, "understanding music in relation to history and culture." I ask the students to research what was going on in our hometown, our state, or our nation when a particular piece of music was written. Once again, they're given a choice of projects they can complete. I've even had students dress in period costumes and write and perform skits about different time periods.

The students are not required to write notes for every piece of music; they only need to choose one. I copy all of the notes, without the authors' names, and the classes vote on which they think should be printed in the program.

Again, I try to give the students options because I want them to enjoy learning about the music and I want them to do a good job on their assignment. I have quite a few students with learning disabilities who would be intimidated by a writing assignment but who would be successful at making a poster about a piece of music. These posters are displayed in my classroom and, of course, at concerts.

Let me talk for just a minute about students with learning disabilities before moving on to Common Core standards. In Illinois, we're all required, in order to keep our certificates up to date, to take courses that address special needs. Yet the information learned by taking these courses is wasted unless you know who needs accommodations. If the special education team at your school has not given you a list of students with individual educational plans, then you need to ask. It's just as important for you to know the best way to help these students as it is for their other academic teachers to know. Music just might be the one class in which they excel, but think how much better they will do if their learning needs are being met.

When you're planning options for completing a project, remember that you also need to create a way to grade them. Chapter 7 is devoted to assessment and the development of rubrics. Don't skip reading it because the title of the chapter is "Assessment." It might well be the most important chapter in the book.

Not only is this your students' chance to use their creativity to learn more about their subject matter, but it's also your chance to do the same. I can almost guarantee that you will find teaching to be a much more rewarding experience, and you, too, might learn something you didn't know before.

COMMON CORE

As of this writing (September 2012), forty-five states, the District of Columbia, Guam, and the U.S. Department of Defense have adopted the Common Core standards. Chances are good that you are already in a school where the curriculum is changing to meet these standards, and if you're not, you probably soon will be.

I'll reserve my diatribe on my philosophy concerning legislated educational edicts, but suffice it to say that I read the Common Core standards through a lens colored heavily with my own skepticism. I was surprised, however, at how much I agreed with them and how easily I could see how music education fits in, particularly with the language arts standards.

According to the Common Core State Standards Initiative website (www.corestandards.org), "The standards set requirements not only for English language arts (ELA) but also for literacy in history/social studies, science, and technical subjects." Since music is widely thought of as a language, it is natural to extend these standards to music curricula. One of the most well-known music educators of the twentieth century, Dr. Shinichi Suzuki, developed an entire methodology for teaching music based on the hypothesis that children learn music the same way that they learn language. Given that premise, let's look at some examples of the language arts Common Core standards.

Under the umbrella of language arts standards there is a specific set of standards for speaking and listening, the first of which reads, "Participate in collaborative conversations with diverse partners about grade (insert grade here) topics and texts with peers and adults in small and larger groups." Under this standard are rules and guidelines for these collaborative discussions. If we look back to the current (1994) National Standards for Music Education that I listed at the beginning of this chapter, do you see how this Common Core standard complements the existing National Standards? Being able to have collaborative, insightful, and educated discussions about the arts (specifically music) is what we would like for our students to be able to do, isn't it?

One of the seventh grade language arts standards reads, "Compare and contrast a written story, drama, or poem to its audio, filmed, staged, or multimedia version, analyzing the effects of techniques unique to each medium (e.g., lighting, sound, color, or camera focus and angles in a film)." This is a real-world application of knowledge: to be able to form an opinion on a work of art and be able to defend that point of view based on observations and knowledge about the media. I would love for my students to be able to intelligently discuss their reasons for liking certain pieces of music, whether they are pop songs, film scores, or symphonies. If we, as music educators, align our curriculum to address Common Core standards such as these, our students will make connections across the curriculum and benefit in so many ways.

The Common Core also has standards for analyzing craft and structure. For instance, in the seventh grade, students should be able to "analyze how a drama's or poem's form or structure contributes to its meaning." In the general music classes I teach, we start talking about form and structure in kindergarten. By seventh grade, students *should* be able to analyze the form and discuss the reasons why a composer might have chosen that particular form. Understanding the form of a piece of music leads to greater understanding. Likewise, understanding that form in music is similar to form in literature leads to greater understanding of both. It's a win-win for your students!

Under the "language" section of Common Core are standards such as these:

- Demonstrate command of the conventions of standard English grammar and usage when writing or speaking.
- Determine a theme or central idea of a text and analyze its development over the course of the text; provide an objective summary of the text.
- Determine the meaning of words and phrases as they are used in a text, including figurative and connotative meanings; analyze the impact of rhymes and other repetitions of sounds (e.g., alliteration) on a specific verse or stanza of a poem or section of a story or drama.
- Analyze how an author develops and contrasts the points of view of different characters or narrators in a text.

There are many more, but can you see how replacing words such as *English grammar* with *standard musical notation* transforms a language standard into a music education standard? Replacing *text* with *sonata*? Replacing *repetition of sounds* with *motifs*? *Author* with *composer*? *Points of view* with *musical themes*? If you have the same expectations for your students in music that the language arts teachers do, everyone wins. Your students understand music better, they understand language better, they learn to make connections between different areas of study, and you gain respect from colleagues and administrators (and perhaps learn something yourself).

If all you do with your performing ensembles is rehearse and perform, your students are missing out on the bigger picture. They're missing out by not contemplating things like the composer's intent, or what music means to them and how it plays a part in their lives—their entire lives, not just the few years that they have in school. Projects that are meaningful to the individual student, authentic, and relevant should be an important and valued facet of your curriculum if you embrace a holistic philosophy of music education.

PHILOSOPHY OF MUSIC EDUCATION—WHAT IS IT, AND WHY DO I NEED ONE?

I finished my undergraduate degree in 1982—practically the neolithic age. The tiny amount of time devoted to philosophy of music education resulted in one three-hundred-word paper that stated my "justification for instrumental music education," written for my senior Instrumental Methods class at the University of Illinois. I still have this paper in a binder on my bookshelf, and I look at it from time to time as a reminder of how ridiculously naïve and shallow I was at age twenty. The sole source for any idea of what a philosophy of music education should be came from chapter 4 of the 1959 book by Charles Leonhard and Robert W. House, *Foundations and Principles of Music Education*.

Although Bennett Reimer had published the first edition of *A Philosophy of Music Education* in 1970 and although he had been on the faculty of the University of Illinois as well as an alumnus, his book was not required reading for undergraduate classes. Our preparation to teach was almost entirely practical in nature, but as I would come to discover, practicality without purpose is pointless, and this is why you as a music teacher must develop your own philosophy of music education. If you only know *how* to do what you're doing, but you're not absolutely clear about *why* you're doing it, it's like trying to find your way to Enid, Oklahoma, without a road map and losing all the passengers in your car along the way.

The word "philosophy" comes from the Greek words *philos* (love) and *sophos* (wisdom), and the love of wisdom is probably the core reason that most good teachers enter the field. However, once in the proverbial trenches, it's easy to get bogged down with procedures, housekeeping, lesson plans, behavior plans, seating charts, and so on. But that's when you need to reflect on your philosophy the most. If you're bogged down and forget why you're teaching, you may as well hang up your baton because you have real human beings relying on you for their collective aesthetic good.

A personal philosophy defines your beliefs about why you teach, what you teach, and how you teach. Developing a philosophy causes you to deeply examine your reasons for doing what you do and enables you to explain and justify them to others. When you are clear about your own philosophy, you are better able to critically analyze methodologies, curricula, and, most importantly, what *you* do with *your* students. This leads not only to higher-level thinking on your part but to higher-level teaching as well.

Post your philosophy on your website. Discuss it. Refine it. But first, you have to write it. The list of books and treatises on music education is long and worth your time, but a good way to begin to form your philosophy is by reading what other music teachers think. If you do an Internet search on music education philosophy, you'll find a vast and varied treasure trove of ideas. Give serious consideration to what you read and build your statement by choosing the bits and pieces that are meaningful to you.

Finally, a reminder that your philosophy should not remain static. The world in which I taught in 1982 is vastly different from the current world of 2013. The students are different. I am different. Schools are different. My philosophy is very different now than it was then. To be an excellent teacher, you must be able to adapt to the needs of your students right now, tomorrow, and for the rest of your career.

SIX

Advocacy

I've touched on the importance of advocacy in the previous chapters, but I'm afraid that some of you might still brush off its importance. I want you to know how to keep what you've worked so hard to build because I know how quickly and easily it might be lost. The fact that you are reading this book at all shows that you're a good teacher and working to become an even better one. Teachers who don't care about their profession don't read books about how to do a better job. Yet all of your effort to build a high-quality music program will be for naught if the school board decides to eliminate it from the available course offerings. That's why part of being a good classroom manager means that you learn how to show off what you do.

If the word around town is that the music classes at your school are absolutely amazing, no one will want to be left out. You can't leave it up to word of mouth, though. You have to go directly to the new prospects and let them know why they should join your ensemble.

More than likely you learned quite a bit about recruiting when you took instrumental or choral methods classes. Remember that you must not only sell the benefits of being in your ensemble to these kids but also sell the kids on you. Dress professionally, but in bright colors. You need to present an authoritative image, but not a boring one.

The first impression your students have of you begins before they ever set foot in your classroom. What they see during a recruiting concert sends a message to potential new students about what you expect of your ensembles, the respect you have for your students, and the respect they have for you. You lay the foundation for a well-managed classroom before you ever get your class.

Let your current ensembles know that playing for incoming students is the most important job they have all year. Without their best performance, the future of the ensemble is at stake. Prepare them to do an absolutely professional but fun presentation. This is the perfect time to program music that younger audiences can recognize. That doesn't necessarily mean Disney show tunes (although don't rule them out), but it could mean arrangements of folk songs they might know or classical music that gets lots of airplay, such as background music for commercials. Theme songs from television programs or cartoons are also good icebreakers.

Involve the prospective students. Invite one of them up to conduct. Ask them questions and give prizes for correct answers. Ask them if they have any questions. Let them know they can be in both band and chorus or orchestra and chorus, or that they can be in both band and sports, if that's possible in your school. If scheduling or the coach's requirements make it impossible for them to do both, then you might have some issues to address with the administration. It's an excellent idea to meet with the coaches of sports that could potentially conflict with your rehearsals and concerts. Usually schedules can be accommodated so that students can participate in both types of activities. If you're willing to compromise a little, the coaches probably will be too.

Have some of your current students speak to recruits about the trips you go on and the other events they participate in during the year. Here's a tip, though: rehearse those speeches. I made the mistake of letting some kids talk without any preparation, and one darling girl told the crowd of fifth graders, "You should take this class; it's an easy A." While it is easy to earn an A in my class if you do what you're supposed to do, it's not really the rationale I want to promote for joining one of my ensembles.

The health of your program depends on your ability to keep new students coming in every year. I know very few music educators who feel completely secure about the future of their programs.

In the district where I live, formerly a quite wealthy school district, the band program was cut last year from the fifth grade, and all band lessons from seventh grade through high school were eliminated. The general music teacher, low on the seniority list, was laid off, and the high school and middle school chorus teachers are now teaching elementary general music. Even within the general music program, cuts were made that eliminated music classes for kindergarten. These cuts came a few years after an initial round of cuts in which the school district terminated the orchestra program, prompting me to start the Prairie Youth Orchestra.

I started the orchestra program in the school where I worked as a general music teacher. At that time, most of the tax revenue in the district was from a nuclear power plant, and the school could fund some pretty wonderful educational programs. However, the electric company fought the assessed valuation of the plant, and the tax assessor decided to cut the value in half. This cut the tax revenue in half, and thus cut the school budget pretty much in half. Cutting that much out of a budget is tough.

The orchestra was not originally slated to be one of the programs to be terminated, but during a late-night public meeting, one of the band directors in the district suggested that orchestra should be cut; nobody there was prepared to present an argument to the contrary. Overnight, the orchestra was gone.

The phone rang off the hook the next day with parents calling to find out what they could do, but it was too late. Another string teacher who lived in the community sat down with me and we came up with a plan for a privately run orchestra that would allow string players who had started playing in the school orchestra program to continue. The Prairie Youth Orchestra was formed and has thrived for the last ten years.

Ironically, the elimination of the orchestra program had a direct effect on the band director who suggested it. Because one of the other band directors was lower on the seniority list than I was, he was laid off, reducing the number of lessons and rehearsals that band students had from then on. Really, all music teachers should work together and develop a curriculum that is symbiotic. Each aspect of the music curriculum is important and beneficial to the other parts. That's another lesson I learned the hard way.

All of this happened in what everyone thought was a very financially stable school district, but when district funds depend on property taxes, one never knows what might happen.

The point is that you need to promote what you do. I know how much you value your program, but do the parents and the members of the community feel the same way? What about your school board and administration? If your program suddenly becomes threatened, are you ready, at a moment's notice, to defend its value?

You and I both know that very few football programs are ever cut from a school budget, and if they are, you can bet that the music program was gone already. The football team is visible. They get publicity. You also need publicity, but the news team won't likely come looking for you; you have to do the reporting yourself. Is that fair? No, but that's the way it is.

Call your local newspaper. Call all of them if you have more than one. Find out who you can contact to advertise your concerts or to recognize your students. Our local paper's editor has an e-mail address, which is so convenient because I can just e-mail her press releases along with pictures taken with a digital camera. Pictures are important. Parents are thrilled to see their little darling's face in the paper, and you become a hero for putting it there. In addition to garnering parental support, pictures also draw attention to the attached article.

Send press releases to announce concerts; fundraising events; community service projects; solo, ensemble, and district festival participants; and any other event that you think deserves some notice. The more often people in your community see the name of your organization, the more important it becomes to them. If, in the future, you need support for your program, you are more likely to have it.

Besides the local papers, you can contact local television and radio stations to see if they might provide community service announcements. Ask how far in advance you need to send it because they often require announcements several weeks prior to the event.

If you have an active parent committee or Music Boosters club, ask if they could designate someone to be your promotions assistant. That person can help make and display posters around town and in schools prior to your concerts and events. They may have contacts in community service clubs that may also spread the word. In fact, you could send groups to play or sing for some of these clubs as another way to get community support.

Performing in venues outside of your school auditorium or gym makes your ensemble much more visible. Offer to have smaller groups perform for Kiwanis luncheons. Play at local businesses during the holidays. I coach small ensembles like trios and quartets so that they can play in stores with limited space. Often, businesses have holiday open houses and are very open to the idea of having local talent perform. It helps draw a crowd for them too. And don't forget—if your group is performing somewhere, send a press release.

Holidays aren't the only time of year to showcase your groups. Of course, if you teach marching band, you perform at parades and athletic events. Our orchestra plays every summer at the kickoff for our town's festival, ByronFest. This requires some summer rehearsals, but we generally choose easy music and the kids enjoy getting together for a few practices before that event. We also have a potluck or swimming party afterward, and it's something everyone looks forward to all year.

Don't overlook the staff in your own school when you promote your performances. Most of the time, they have no idea when your concerts are scheduled and never would have thought to ask. This is why posters should be put up inside your school building to advertise the performance. As I mentioned earlier, the concert that had the highest attendance on record for my groups was the one in which we had one of the sixth-grade teachers singing a solo. He won the vote-for-a-teacher-to-sing-a-solo contest that was part of our community service project. Obviously, the kids and staff loved him because he received ten times more votes than the next-highest candidate. Staff and non-music students alike came to the concert just to hear him sing four measures.

In my district, the principal is required to be at the concerts. It's nice, though, to send a personal invitation from you or, better yet, from the kids. Also, send invitations to the superintendent and members of the board of education. After all, these are people who may decide sometime in the future whether you still have a job, or whether your school has music at all.

Everything you do all year long influences how well you can convince kids that they should be part of your organization. Once those students are on your rosters, each facet of your management plan plays a part in the overall success of your ensembles. The more control you have over daily events in your classroom, the easier it is to impart your knowledge to the eager sponges that are your students.

Now you can teach technique, music history, appreciation, theory, phrasing, musicality, improvisation—all the reasons you became a music educator in the first place. Remember these keys to success:

1. Devise a plan. Every good classroom manager has a plan before a single student sets foot in the classroom. The plan is multifaceted and all aspects are thought out with an end product in mind. Included in this plan are philosophy, classroom organization, behavior, communication, curriculum, assessment, and advocacy.
2. Set the plan in motion. Implement your plan in an organized and deliberate manner. You've worked hard to get everything ready; make sure you follow your own outline for success, step by step.
3. Stick to your plan. Don't allow your students or their parents to steer you off course. Keep track of your goals—daily, weekly, monthly, quarterly—and you'll have an easier time redirecting your class if it starts to head in the wrong direction.
4. Be unswerving and don't let up. When things are running smoothly, it's easy to become lax in our efforts to maintain a behavior plan. Make sure that all infractions of your rules are addressed at all times during the school year. Your students will have much more respect for you if you're fair and consistent.
5. Reevaluate your plan. This isn't going to work perfectly and be error-free the first time out. Test-drive your original plan and make corrections when it's logical to do so. The respect your students have for you deteriorates if you make random changes. Even alterations have to be done in an unbiased, systematic manner.
6. Create a team. The definition of the word symphony is "something that is harmoniously composed of various elements." That should describe each one of your ensembles. Everyone benefits if you have groups that work well together. Students have a richer, more meaningful musical experience. They learn more from you and from each other. Your audiences will enjoy concerts that are inspiring and exciting because ensembles that work together also perform that way. In addition, you receive more of a payoff than you ever imagined possible when you know the joy of directing an ensemble that truly understands the word "symphony."
7. Show off! Once you have all of this in place, your hard work is not over. You must work hard to keep what you have and to keep it growing from year to year. Learn to be your own press agent and

manager. Make your program visible in the community and organize an advocacy group that is prepared at any moment to defend what you do.

It will get easier from year to year after you've worked to develop your original plan, but it will always be a system in flux. I think you'll find, though, that you can be much more creative when you have a structure in place that works as an outline for all you do.

SEVEN

Assessment

Why have I devoted an entire chapter to assessment in a book about classroom management? Report cards are part of the job, and you need to be as prepared and organized as possible when you give grades. A big part of good classroom management is giving fair and objective grades that you can support with documented evaluations. These days, when schools and teachers have to be more accountable than ever, you need to be able to show that you have objectives aligned with the National Standards for Music Education and that you are meeting them. For most music educators, the assessment part of the job doesn't come naturally. We're artists, not bookkeepers, right? But even artists have to keep the books, or they're in trouble.

Unlike academic classes, assessments in performance-based classes, for the most part, are not done with written tests. You might include written tests as part of the overall curriculum, but the focus of performance-based classes is, well . . . performance! Grades should reflect students' participation and ability to perform.

I admit it. For the first decade of my teaching career, I gave grades based on behavior. If kids weren't a behavior problem and they participated in my class, they'd get an A. But those days are over, my friend. When a parent comes into my office and asks why his or her child got a C, I need to be able to show how I systematically arrived at that grade. When my principal or superintendent requests a copy of my objectives and asks how the state or National Standards are addressed, I have to be able to produce evidence quickly and impressively.

Shoddy assessment procedures are irresponsible on several levels. First of all, if you do not address the National Standards for Music Education and assess how well your students are doing, you shortchange music education as a whole. If you do what I did (grading on behavior), you're probably not taking your profession seriously enough. I say that with a lot of compassion because, as I said before, that's exactly what I did for at least ten years before I saw the assessment light. Music should be part of every child's education in this country and should be taken as seriously as any other subject in the curriculum.

Second, you're in danger of losing your career if you aren't up to snuff where assessment is concerned. If you don't treat music education as an academic subject, then the administration, parents, and (most importantly) your students won't either. It's a part of classroom management. The more effort and organization you put into what you do, the more you get back from your students, their parents, and the administration.

What follows is a step-by-step system of evaluation and assessment that is relatively simple to use. Once you have it in place, it is flexible and adjustable so that you don't have to spend hours and hours rewriting standards, objectives, and rubrics when you make changes to your curriculum. You will spend some time at the beginning setting things up, but when you change or add to your curriculum, you can just plug the new stuff right into the existing framework.

NATIONAL STANDARDS

Until new standards are published, you can obtain a copy of the National Association for Music Education's National Standards for Music Education. Every set of state and local standards that I've come across either imitates this list or is less comprehensive, so if you use these standards, you've pretty much covered all your bases. NAfME's national standards are as follows:

1. Singing, alone and with others, a varied repertoire of music
2. Performing on instruments, alone and with others, a varied repertoire of music
3. Improvising melodies, variations, and accompaniments
4. Composing and arranging music within specified guidelines
5. Reading and notating music
6. Listening to, analyzing, and describing music
7. Evaluating music and music performances
8. Understanding relationships between music, the other arts, and disciplines outside the arts
9. Understanding music in relation to history and culture

Do you need to cover all of those standards in your classroom every day? No. Every year? Yes. Depending on what you teach, you will address one or more of them every day. Band and orchestra students perform on instruments alone and with others quite frequently, but do band and orchestra teachers have their students sing every day? Maybe some of them do, but I doubt singing happens very often in a band or orchestra rehearsal. Do choir students use instruments every day? No, but they will need to use them every once in a while. See what I mean?

Get a notebook for each different class that you teach. Write one of the content standards at the top of a page and make your list of activities underneath. Think about what you teach and what you want your students to learn, and then go through and write down everything that you do that falls under each standard. It's likely at first that you might have some empty spaces under some of the standards. That's where you need to challenge yourself to create activities, projects, and lessons to address those areas.

One of my lists for middle school chorus looks like this:

Singing, Alone and with Others, a Varied Repertoire of Music

- Sight-singing practice and evaluations (singing alone)
- Individual evaluation on performance music (singing alone, varied repertoire)
- Rehearsal and performance of concert music including "Kye Kye Kule" (African), "Didn't My Lord Deliver Daniel" (American spiritual), "Hawaiian Rollercoaster Ride" (American movie soundtrack), and "Ave Verum Corpus" (classical era Western, Mozart)
- Small ensemble performances at Miracle on 2nd Street (holiday music)
- Performance at ByronFest (patriotic music)

Let's say you're an orchestra teacher, though, and you have no activities listed under Standard 1 ("singing, alone and with others, a varied repertoire of music"). How do you address that situation? Of course, you realize that singing is a terrific way to develop intonation sensitivity when teaching instrumental music, right? How often do you have your students sing their parts? They can sing them in solfège, or they could make up words to go along with the music that they play, or they could simply sing the pitches on any given syllable, like *la*. For the same content standard, the page in your notebook might look like this for orchestra or band:

Singing, Alone and with Others, a Varied Repertoire of Music

- Practice in sectional rehearsals singing melodic phrases chosen from performance music (singing, with others, varied repertoire)
- Individual vocal performance of rehearsed passages with students singing on the syllable *la* (singing, alone)
- Warm-up exercises, singing for audiation (singing, with others)

If one group is singing a passage, then perhaps another section of the orchestra could make up an ostinato to go along with it to emphasize the tonic and dominant. Wow! Now you have an activity that encompasses both Standard 1 and Standard 4. Guess what else? Your students also develop a better understanding of the music. Now that's creative teaching!

Check with other teachers you know to see what they're doing. Ask if they have any new ideas for incorporating all of the National Standards into their curricula. Go to conferences and take classes that address the National Standards and learning objectives. Do a search on the Internet for music lesson plans; zillions of them are available to spark your imagination.

ASSESSMENT

That list of activities that you make is the first step in organizing what you teach so that you can figure out how to assess the students' performance in each area. Do you have to assess every student every single time he or she does something that falls under one of the National Standards? Of course not. I choose two or three standards to assess each quarter so that each student is evaluated on all nine standards at some time during the school year.

For instance, during the first quarter of school, I evaluate my students' abilities to read and notate music, addressing Standard 9. I probably assess this skill almost daily, but I do a formal evaluation during the first quarter. During that same grading period, I also do my formal assessment of Standard 1, "singing, alone and with others, a varied repertoire of music." I like to get an initial evaluation for those two standards at the beginning of the year and at the end of the year to see how far each student has progressed. By choosing two or three standards to assess each quarter, I can spend more time on each lesson and still use the majority of my class time for rehearsing music.

After making a list of the lessons or activities that you do, choose one lesson for each standard that you will use for assessment at some point in the year. It might work out that you have a whole bunch of activities for some standards and only one or two for others. When starting out, choose one assessment each year for each standard and for each class that you teach. Once you get more organized and become accustomed to doing the actual evaluations and recordkeeping, it will be easier to add more later if you want to or need to.

In your notebook, go through each page and circle the activity you would most like to use to evaluate your students' progress. Next, write an objective for that activity. In other words, what do you want students to be able to do as a result of that task? What could they do that would show you that they understand and have mastery of what you are asking them to do?

You probably spent hours in college writing objectives, but that was back when they were for hypothetical students instead of real ones. Now you have real students and maybe you've forgotten how to write an objective. It's simple: Start with the words, "As a result of this activity, the student should be able to _______." Think of a verb to fill in the blank that fits what you want to do, such as "sing" or "play." Be careful not to use the words "know" or "understand" because they are too vague. You can't see a student knowing or understanding, but you can see them playing or singing.

Now, under what conditions should the student be able to perform the given task? With music? Without music? Alone or in a small group? With the teacher present or recorded? These conditions are all up to you, but you must be specific. Here's a page from my assessment notebook:

Ninth-Grade Orchestra

Content Standard 1: Singing, alone and with others, a varied repertoire of music.

Objective: As a result of repeated practice in class, the student will sing alone for the teacher the primary and secondary melody of the fugue from Vivaldi's Concerto Grosso in D minor using the syllable *la*. Students will read from their music.

I address the first National Standard by having my ninth-grade orchestra students sing the primary and secondary melodies from a fugue after we practiced them during class. The verb used in this objective is "sing." Singing is something that can easily be observed. The conditions are that, using their music, the student will sing alone for the teacher on the syllable *la*.

Next, decide what you consider mastery of the objective. I love rubrics for this, and I never thought I would say I love rubrics. I'm a former rubric hater. In the 1990s, "rubric" was a big buzzword in education. I heard the word all the time, and I think I hated it because I didn't know what it meant. I still wish they'd find a different word, but I did learn what rubrics are, so I'm a little more comfortable with them now. A rubric is basically a scoring tool that helps you define your criteria for evaluating a student's work. Rubrics simplified my life by allowing me to structure how I assess my students. Grading is no longer an ambiguous process for me. I have evidence of whether or not a student has gained mastery of the skills I think he or she should have after going through my curriculum.

You can take entire classes just to learn how to design rubrics if you want, but, for the time being, you simply need to think about what exactly you consider to be mastery, partial mastery, or non-mastery of the objective that you have written for your students. Here are four steps to creating a rubric:

1. Choose the precise skill that you want to assess. Depending on the level of complexity of the skill, you may have a rubric with just one particular component that you are grading, or you might have a rubric that has many sections. Think about the judges' grading sheets for solo and ensemble contests. They have a point value for rhythm, one for intonation, one for stage presence, and so on. Are you evaluating the student's overall performance on an excerpt or just the rhythm? Be specific. Decide what exactly you are assessing.
2. Decide what you consider to be mastery of the skill, partial mastery, or non-mastery, and assign a range of point values to each category. Let's say I have a chorus student who is sight-singing for the first time in sixth grade and sings a four-measure quarter-note-only melody consisting of the following pitches: *sol, mi, la,* and *do.* I would define mastery of the skill as singing nearly every pitch and interval correctly. A student with partial mastery would be singing many of the pitches and intervals correctly and his or her voice would at least be moving in the same direction as the notes on the staff. A student who demonstrates non-mastery would be a student who sang pitches moving downward when they should have moved upward, and so on. Each category would have a range of points. For instance, the student would receive an "A" for mastery with a score of ten for no errors at all, nine for one error, and eight for two errors. I would give a "B" or "C" for partial mastery with a point range of three through eight, and a "D" or "F" for non-mastery with a point range of zero to two points.
3. Use language that defines exactly what constitutes the level of mastery of the skill. For instance, if a student plays a scale and you're developing a rubric for intonation, is mastery the ability to perform every note in tune, or seven out of eight notes in tune?

After you define what you consider mastery of the skill, use language that conveys this meaning so that students and their parents understand precisely how you arrived at their scores. For instance, on the scoring sheet you can write something like the following:

A (mastery): Seven to eight notes out of eight are played in tune
B (partial mastery): Five to six notes are played in tune
C (partial mastery): Three to four notes are played in tune
D (non-mastery): One to two notes are played in tune
F (non-mastery): Zero notes are played in tune

4. Make sure that your rubric is reliable. This is where trial and error comes in. Even if you think you've developed a phenomenal rubric for the skill you want to assess, you might find some bugs to work out when you put it into practice. It's okay to adjust things so that the rubric works better. Once you have developed a rubric that works well, save it!

For example, here's what the rubric looks like that I use for the objective of singing the fugue melodies from Vivaldi's Concerto Grosso:

A (92–100 points, mastery): Zero to four mistakes in either rhythm or pitch.
B (86–91 points, near mastery): Three to five mistakes in rhythm. Most pitches and intervals are correct. Melodic direction matches the direction of the music.
C (78–85 points, partial mastery): Six to nine mistakes in rhythm. Melodic direction matches the direction of the music.
D (70–77 points, improving partial mastery): Rhythm is almost entirely incorrect. Melodic direction matches the direction of the music.
F (69 or less points, non-mastery): Rhythm is almost entirely or is entirely incorrect. Melodic direction does not match the direction of the music.

Note the definitions of mastery in each category. I prefer that these statements sound positive, if at all possible. It may take some trial and error and some adjusting of your rubric before you really learn what works, but that's all right. You have to start somewhere. The Rubistar website, located at http://rubistar.4teachers.org, is an excellent resource for teachers and has a fabulous rubric tool. You can enter your information in a very easy-to-use format and then print out your rubrics. This is a great way to get started.

Now your notebook should look something like this on each page:

Ninth-Grade Orchestra

Content Standard 1: Singing, alone and with others, a varied repertoire of music.

Activities

Practice in sectional rehearsals singing melodic phrases chosen from performance music (singing, with others, a varied repertoire)

Individual vocal performance of rehearsed passages with students singing on the syllable *la* (singing, alone)—assess this activity second quarter

Warm-up exercises, singing for audiation (singing, with others)

Objective: The student will sing the fugue primary and secondary melody from Vivaldi's Concerto Grosso in D minor using the syllable *la*.

Rubric

A (92–100 points, mastery): Zero to four mistakes in either rhythm or pitch.

B (86–91 points, near mastery): Three to five mistakes in rhythm. Most pitches and intervals are correct. Melodic direction matches the direction of the music.

C (78–85 points, partial mastery): Six to nine mistakes in rhythm. Melodic direction matches the direction of the music.

D (70–77 points, improving partial mastery): Rhythm is almost entirely incorrect. Melodic direction matches the direction of the music.

F (69 or less points, non-mastery): Rhythm is almost entirely or is entirely incorrect. Melodic direction does not match the direction of the music.

Finally, decide when during the year the activity that addresses this objective and its assessment will take place. If you're like me, you program most of your music for the year's concerts before the school year starts. If you're not like me, allow me suggest to you that it might be a good idea to do that. It's easy to adjust, add, or remove music, but it sure helps to start with a plan. You can save time by ordering all the music at once, you can plan themes for your programs (if you like doing that), and you can make sure your curriculum happens sequentially.

Spacing out assessments is important. You don't want to forget to do them until May and then spend the entire month testing your students. You won't like it, and believe me, your students won't like it either. I don't know about you, but I'd rather prepare for concerts and contests in the spring than catch up on all the evaluations I should have been doing all year. Plan ahead and that won't happen.

After you've planned your curriculum, aligned it with the National Standards, developed rubrics, and assessed the skills of your students, make sure that your administrators and parents see and understand what you're doing. Curriculum development garners respect from your academic peers (the other teachers in the building who don't teach music), the parents of your students, and the administration. The quality of your curriculum helps to enable others to view music education less as an extracurricular activity and more as an integral part of a child's overall education. It is vital that we, as music teachers, take our profession as seriously as do the teachers of math, science, and English. A comprehensive plan for meeting the National Standards is vital in order to validate what we know is true: music education is an essential component of a child's schooling.

In these days of rapidly advancing technology and political overtures of educational reform, the inclusion of music in the curricula of American schools has to be based on the values of music as they apply to the goals of our overall educational system. Due to changing technology, new classes are getting added to the school day, and once again, the fine arts are threatened. We must be diligent in our effort to promote our discipline. We have a responsibility to be the best educators we can be and to provide a high-quality music education for our students.

You have a responsibility to organize and manage your classroom and your curriculum to provide the best possible music education to your students. The time you spend preparing to teach is as important as the time you spend in front of your class.

In a speech at General Dynamics in San Diego, Gus Grissom, a Mercury astronaut, spoke to a group of spacecraft assemblers working on the rocket that would carry him into space. "Do good work," was all he said. Grissom knew the importance of those assembly workers. They had his life in their hands. That simple phrase became the slogan for the project team. Huge banners and posters were put up and special tags were attached to Mercury parts. All boasted the motto "Do good work!"

You have the educational welfare of your students in your hands. Concise and yet profoundly eloquent, the same message now goes out to you. Do good work.

Appendix A: Sample Choral Handbook

Welcome back to school! The following contains important information about the choral program at Meridian Junior High School and the upcoming year. Students and parents need to read it over carefully and then sign and return the signature page before Friday, August 31.

AREAS OF FOCUS

- Musical literacy—reading pitch and rhythm
- Knowledge of musical styles and related world and music history
- Performance skills—vocal technique, diction, ear-training, and sight-singing

PERFORMANCE SCHEDULE

- Fall Choral Concert, Tuesday, October 9, 7:00 p.m.**
- IMEA Auditions in Sterling (grades 7 and 8; optional), Saturday, October 16
- IMEA District Festival in DeKalb, Saturday, November 13 (audition winners only)
- Winter Choral Concert, Tuesday, December 14, 7:00 p.m.**
- Route 72 Solo and Ensemble Contest, Saturday, February 5, at Aplington Middle School
- Route 72 Organizational Contest, Thursday, March 17, at Byron Middle School**
- Spring Choral Concert, Tuesday, May 25, 7:00 p.m.**
- In the Parks Competition at Six Flags Great America, Friday, May 28

**Required Performance

OTHER IMPORTANT NOTES

A holiday performance will take place at CherryVale Mall in December. This is optional, will most likely occur on a Sunday afternoon in December, and will require parent transportation.

The third annual Ladies' Day fundraiser will tentatively take place on Saturday, April 28. This is a fundraiser to defray the cost of the Music in the Parks competition. Everyone going is expected to participate in this fundraiser.

A music department trip will be planned for the spring. We have attended Broadway musicals in Chicago for the last two years and hope to do so again this year but are awaiting announcement of the spring season.

ENSEMBLE BEHAVIOR

Our choral ensembles are essentially music teams. The actions of any individual can either help or hinder the entire ensemble in both rehearsal and performance. Self-discipline is not optional; it is required. Repeat offenders will be removed from the class at the director's discretion.

A system of checks and warnings will be used to promote proper ensemble behavior. Students will receive a check mark for any infraction in the following areas:

- Prepared for class
- In seat and quiet when the bell rings
- Quiet during rehearsal when not singing
- Demonstrates correct posture while singing
- Respect for self and others
- Participates appropriately during rehearsal

Each week,

- One check mark will result in a verbal warning from the teacher and a five-point subtraction from the quarterly grade.
- Two check marks will result in disqualification from weekly class reward drawing and a ten-point subtraction from the quarterly grade.
- Three check marks will result in a detention and a twenty-five-point subtraction from the quarterly grade.

GRADING

Grades are earned through my assessment of each student's knowledge (classroom assignments, quizzes, and exams), skills (sight-singing and ear-training assessments), and participation in daily rehearsals and required performances. Grades will be assessed on a point system as follows:

- Rehearsals (five points per rehearsal)
- Classroom assignments and quizzes (one hundred points per quarter)—may include oral and written tests and assignments
- Performance attendance (two hundred points per performance)

1. The performance of the chorus is the primary function of the class; therefore, attendance is required.
2. Written excuses may be considered when submitted two weeks prior to the concert if the excuse has validity.
3. Unexcused absences for performances will result in no points being issued for that performance.
4. Students must wear the appropriate concert dress for performances. Failure to be properly attired will result in a deduction of fifty points.
5. If the concert is missed due to an excused absence (sick on day of performance or approval by director), a makeup essay will be assigned and will be due within three days of the student's return to school.

Grading Scale

400–500 points each quarter: A
300–399 points each quarter: B
200–299 points each quarter: C
100–199 points each quarter: D
0–99 points each quarter: F

PERFORMANCES

As this is a performance-based class, attendance at all performances is mandatory. The dates and places are listed above. Please put these dates on your calendar now so that you can schedule around them. Why is attendance mandatory at performances?

- Performing for an audience is the primary focus of this class. Concerts provide an experience that cannot be reproduced in the classroom.
- Performances are the means by which the skills learned in class are evaluated.
- Choral singing is a group effort. The performance is weakened by every missing voice. We rehearse together and we perform together.

PROCEDURES AND ROUTINES

- Be on time and in your assigned seat when the bell rings.
- Participate in all classroom activities—especially singing!
- Be prepared! Have your folder of music, a pencil, and a notebook with you for every class.
- No food, gum, or soft drinks are allowed. Water is permitted.

CONCERT DRESS

Black shoes and socks, black pants, and concert T-shirt are required. The T-shirts will be ordered mid-September and will be approximately $8. The same shirt is used for band and chorus and is the same one used last year.

IMPORTANT!

Read and discuss this entire handbook with your child before signing and returning the signature page.

Please return the completed signature page to Mrs. Haugland before Friday, August 31. Make sure to keep the concert schedule and mark the dates on your calendar now. If any changes occur, you will be notified as soon as possible.

SIGNATURE PAGE

I have read the choral handbook and understand the expectations. If I have any questions or concerns, I will contact Mrs. Haugland.

Student Signature ________________________________
Parent/Guardian Signature ________________________________

Appendix B: Sample Blank Checkbook Page

Week of: ________________

Name	*In seat when bell rings*	*Prepared for class*	*Proper posture*	*Quiet during rehearsal*	*Shows respect for self and others*	*Participates appropriately*	*Goes above and beyond*

Appendix C: Ideas for Student Projects

- Compose variations on a theme.
- Create a pictorial timeline of events in a composer's life.
- Create a poster showing historical events relating to a composition.
- Write an essay describing the musical qualities of a composition.
- Write program notes for a concert performance.
- Write and perform a skit in which a composer is being interviewed.
- Draw a graphic representation of a specific musical form.
- Use a Venn diagram to compare and contrast two different compositions.
- Create a mobile to illustrate historical events relating to a composition.
- Write and perform a skit in which a news anchor reports on a new composition.
- Create *Jeopardy!* or other game show questions about a composer or piece of music.
- Create a board game that tracks the musical form of a composition.
- Create a Web page about a composer or a specific piece of music.

Appendix D: Sample Rubrics

HIGH SCHOOL BAND SIGHT-READING RUBRIC

Note: Students will be given one minute to review the excerpt before they play.

Rating criteria:

Pitch

2—Student plays all of the pitches correctly
1—Student plays the majority of the pitches correctly
0—Student plays fewer than half of the pitches correctly

Rhythm

2—Student plays all of the rhythms correctly
1—Student plays the majority of the rhythms correctly
0—Student plays fewer than half of the rhythms correctly

Articulation

2—Student plays all of the articulations correctly
1—Student plays the majority of the articulations correctly
0—Student plays fewer than half of the articulations correctly

Dynamics

2—Student performs all of the dynamics printed in the music
1—Student performs some of the dynamics printed in the music
0—Student performs none of the dynamics printed in the music

Tempo

2—Student plays at the appropriate tempo throughout the excerpt
1—Student plays at the appropriate tempo throughout most of the excerpt
0—Student does not play at the appropriate tempo

Total Score

9–10 points: A
7–8 points: B
5–6 points: C
3–4 points: D
0–2 points: F

MIDDLE SCHOOL OR HIGH SCHOOL INSTRUMENTAL OR VOCAL PERFORMANCE EVALUATION

Student Name:
Purpose of the Assessment:
Evaluator: 6 (98 percent), 5 (90 percent), 4 (75 percent), 3 (50 percent), 2 (30 percent), 1 (less than 30 percent)

Rhythm accuracy	_____
Tone quality	_____
Pitch accuracy	_____
Articulation or diction	_____
Musicianship	_____
Total points	_____

Total score:

27–30 points: A
23–26 points: B
19–22 points: C
15–18 points: D
0–14 points: F

CHORAL PERFORMANCE EVALUATION

Rating criteria:

Pitch

2—Student sings all pitches accurately
1—Student sings most pitches accurately
0—Student sings few pitches accurately

Rhythm

2—Student sings all rhythms accurately
1—Student sings most rhythms accurately
0—Student sings few rhythms accurately

Intonation

2—Student sings all pitches in tune
1—Student sings most pitches in tune
0—Student sings few pitches in tune

Tone Quality

2—Student sings beautifully, focused
1—Student sings pleasantly, moderately focused
0—Student produces poor tone

Breath Support

2—Student has excellent breath support
1—Student has average breath support
0—Student has little or no breath support

Diction

2—Student sings excellent consonant attacks and releases
1—Some of the text is indistinct
0—Text is not understandable

Projection

2—Student projects a full, pleasing tone
1—Student projects a moderate volume
0—Student is inaudible

Total Score

12–14 points: A
9–11 points: B
6–8 points: C
5–7 points: D
0–4 points: F

Appendix E: Resources

SUGGESTED READING

Boonshaft, P. L. 2002. *Teaching Music with Passion: Conducting, Rehearsing, and Inspiring*. Galesville, Md.: Meredith Music.

Consortium of National Arts Associations. 1994. *National Standards for Arts Education: What Every Young American Should Know and Be Able to Do in the Arts*. Reston, Va.: MENC: The National Association for Music Education.

Conway, C. M., and T. M. Hodgman. 2006. *Handbook for the Beginning Music Teacher*. Chicago: GIA Publications.

Hal Leonard Corporation. 2005. *The Music Director's Cookbook: Creative Recipes for a Successful Program*. Galesville, Md.: Meredith Music.

Jones, A. 2000. *Team-Building Activities for Every Group*. Richland, Wash.: Rec Room Publishing.

Kagan, L., M. Kagan, and S. Kagan. 1997. *Cooperative Learning Structures for Teambuilding*. San Clemente, Calif.: Kagan Cooperative Learning.

Lindeman, C. A., ed. 2003. *Benchmarks in Action: A Guide to Standards Based Assessment*. Reston, Va.: MENC: The National Association for Music Education.

MENC: The National Association for Music Education. 1989. *Music Booster Manual*. Reston, Va.: Author.

———. 1991. *Building Support for School Music*. Reston, Va.: Author.

———. 2004. *Teacher to Teacher: A Music Educator's Survival Guide*. Reston, Va.: Author.

Reimer, B. 2000. *Performing with Understanding: The Challenge of National Standards for Music Education*. Reston, Va.: MENC: The National Association for Music Education.

Rossman, R. L., ed. 1989. *TIPS: Discipline in the Music Classroom*. Reston, Va.: MENC: The National Association for Music Education.

ADVOCACY WEBSITES

www.nammfoundation.org
www.childrensmusicworkshop.com/advocacy/index.html
www.isme.org
http://advocacy.nafme.org
www.musiceducationonline.org
www.schoolmusicmatters.com
www.supportmusic.com
www.vh1.com/partners/save_the_music

About the Author

Susan L. Haugland received her bachelor's degree in music education from the University of Illinois at Urbana–Champaign and her master's degree in music education from Boston University; she is also the recipient of a music education fellowship at Northwestern University. She has taught elementary general music in grades K–5, orchestra and band in grades 4–12, and middle school chorus. She currently teaches elementary general music and orchestra in Lake Bluff School District #65 in Lake Bluff, Illinois.